Botticelli in the Fire & Fire

Sunday in Sodom

ALSO BY JORDAN TANNAHILL

PLAYS

Age of Minority: Three Solo Plays
Late Company
Concord Floral
Declarations

FICTION

Liminal

NON-FICTION

Theatre of the Unimpressed: In Search of Vital Drama
The Videofag Book (edited with William Ellis)

Botticelli in the & Fire

Sunday in Sodom

Two plays by
Jordan Tannahill

PLAYWRIGHTS CANADA PRESS
TORONTO

For professional or amateur production rights, please contact:
Colin Rivers, Marquis Entertainment
312-73 Richmond St. W., Toronto, ON M5H 4E8
416.960.9123, info@marquisent.ca, www.marquisent.ca

LIBRARY AND ARCHIVES CANADA CATALOGUING IN PUBLICATION
Tannahill, Jordan
[Plays. Selections]
    Botticelli in the fire ; &, Sunday in Sodom / Jordan Tannahill.

Plays.
Issued in print and electronic formats.
ISBN 978-1-77091-917-4 (softcover).--ISBN 978-1-77091-918-1 (PDF).--
ISBN 978-1-77091-919-8 (EPUB).--ISBN 978-1-77091-920-4 (Kindle)

    I. Tannahill, Jordan . Botticelli in the fire. II. Tannahill, Jordan .
Sunday in Sodom. III. Title.

PS8639.A577A6 2018   C812'.6   C2018-903580-3
                                                    C2018-903581-1

Playwrights Canada Press acknowledges that we operate on land which, for thousands of years, has been the traditional territories of the Mississaugas of the New Credit, the Huron-Wendat, the Anishinaabe, Métis, and Haudenosaunee people. Today, this meeting place is home to many Indigenous peoples from across Turtle Island and we are grateful to have the opportunity to work and play here.

We acknowledge the financial support of the Canada Council for the Arts—which last year invested $153 million to bring the arts to Canadians throughout the country—the Ontario Arts Council (OAC), Ontario Creates, and the Government of Canada for our publishing activities.

Canada Council
for the Arts
Conseil des arts
du Canada

ONTARIO ARTS COUNCIL
CONSEIL DES ARTS DE L'ONTARIO
an Ontario government agency
un organisme du gouvernement de l'Ontario

Canada

ONTARIO
CREATES
ONTARIO
CRÉATIF

Dedicated to Saint Genet and Saint Jarman

PLAYWRIGHT'S NOTE

A few years ago I came across a footnote in an art-history textbook that mentioned Sandro Botticelli—the famed painter of pagan imagery in the early Renaissance—burned several of his lost masterpieces at a bonfire of the vanities in 1497. The bonfire was a massive inferno of books, paintings, musical instruments, and all manner of "occasions of sin" orchestrated by the charismatic friar Girolamo Savonarola in reaction to the emergence of secular thought and the Renaissance. Many historians believe that Botticelli was genuinely swayed by the friar's firebrand teachings, but *Botticelli in the Fire* goes about queering the official record, providing an alternate rationale for his drastic action. Both Sandro Botticelli and Leonardo da Vinci were accused of sodomy in their lifetimes; an offence that saw many men burned at the pyre throughout Italy at the time. The play asks: In a moment of great social unrest and political upheaval, in which sodomites were the scapegoat du jour, what deals with the devil were made to avoid the fire? *Botticelli in the Fire* aims to be both a meditation on the ways in which, throughout history, pleasure, sexuality, and "vice" are blamed for all manner of ills, as well as a celebration of the enduring spirit of queer survival.

The parallels between 1497 and the present have only grown more stark since the play's Toronto premiere, and resonated in chilling, new ways when performed mere blocks from Capitol Hill in Washington, DC, in May 2018. A people's fury at an entrenched and unresponsive ruling class, the rise of an incendiary populism, the vilification of minorities and metropolitans, the assailing of art. In this new age of upheaval, I can't help but wonder, with immense apprehension, what forms the bonfires of tomorrow will take.

Sunday in Sodom, on the other hand, is a feminist retelling of the mythic destruction of Sodom and Gomorrah as told by Lot's wife; a story recounted in the holy books of all three Abrahamic faiths. In the Bible she is unnamed, mentioned in a single sentence when she is turned to a pillar of salt for looking back at the destruction of her hometown. When I was growing up, my father read the Bible to my brother and I as a bedtime story each night. The story of Lot's wife was seared into my consciousness at a very young age. I tried to imagine what went through her mind as she decided to disobey god and turn back to behold his wrath. I would try to imagine her face. Sometimes I would imagine her as my own mother. In *Sunday in Sodom* her name is Edith, and she recounts that final, fateful day, in a town that is situated both within a mythic, Biblical past and an all-too-real contemporary present.

What is a sodomite? Who gets to tell their story? And for what end? After centuries of being spoken for and about, maligned, maimed, and misremembered, it's time for the sodomites to speak for themselves.

—Jordan Tannahill

NOTATION

An em dash (—) at the end of a line denotes a cut-off.

An em dash (—) at the start of a line denotes a carry-through of a previous line.

A forward slash (/) denotes the place where the next line begins, causing overlap.

Line breaks suggest spoken rhythm and internal microshifts of thought.

Text in the right-hand column is meant to be spoken in overlap with text on the left.

Occasionally lines run longer than the page width, and continue indented in the line below. These lines are meant to be performed as single, continuous thoughts, without break.

Botticelli in the Fire

RE-IMAGINING HISTORY
by Kirsten Bowen, Production Dramaturg

In February 1497, Florence was burning as followers of conservative Dominican friar Girolamo Savonarola created a massive sixty-foot, seven-storey pile of luxuries—heretical and immoral books, nude paintings, musical instruments, perfumes, and baubles—and lit them on fire. This bonfire of the vanities may have also contained artwork by the painter Sandro Botticelli. Why did Botticelli participate? And why did he save his most famous and notorious painting, *The Birth of Venus*?

Answers to these questions are posited by Jordan Tannahill in *Botticelli in the Fire*, which, though inspired by real people, is a historical reimagining that has as much to say about our world today as five hundred years ago.

Tannahill first wrote the play as a companion piece to *Sunday in Sodom*, which is a contemporary update of the story of Lot's wife, answering another ancient mystery of why she turned around. Toronto's Canadian Stage premiered both pieces on the same bill in 2016. Tannahill's initial inspiration for both plays was to present them from the points of view of those who have been typically left out of the story. He is interested in these "alternate histories," from a different, up until now untold, perspective.

In the case of *Botticelli in the Fire*, Tannahill re-examines history from a queer lens. "What are the narratives that have been buried through time and silenced?" he has asked. "I'm interested in excavating those or queering existing narratives."

In their 2005 essay "Queering History," Jonathan Goldberg and Madhavi Menon write,

In opposition to a historicism that proposes to know the definitive difference between the past and the present, we venture that queering requires what we might term "unhistoricism." Far from being ahistorical—or somehow outside history—unhistoricism would acknowledge that history as it is hegemonically understood today is inadequate to housing the project of queering . . . To queer the Renaissance would thus mean not only looking for alternative sexualities in the past but also challenging the methodological orthodoxy by which past and present are constrained and straitened; it would mean resisting the strictures of knowability itself . . .*

In other words, to queer history opens up not only the parameters of sexual identity, but how we see and understand history itself.

For Tannahill, "Queerness is about taking a sense of power and ownership over being on the periphery. It's a joyous, radical space in which to dismantle and question the status quo." Tannahill's history of Sandro Botticelli presents him as a queer artist and celebrity whose appetite for life and art know no bounds, even as he and his community are threatened by a deadly plague and persecution as "sodomites."

To tell this story, Tannahill has accelerated and smashed together historical events and brought together historical figures in new and invented contexts. This version has Botticelli himself greeting us from beyond the grave to tell the story of his downfall. He begins with the commissioning of *The Birth of Venus* by his patron Lorenzo de' Medici; his relationship with his assistant and mentee Leonardo da Vinci; and the rise of Savonarola, who is determined to bring the rich, powerful, and decadent of Florence to their knees, including the artists whom they support.

Tannahill's retelling does not stop with altering the historic record, but brings that history into closer conversation with the present. Characters speak in casual, contemporary vernacular, and anachronisms abound, from cellphones to limousines. Thus early Renaissance Florence—a city of wealth and opportunity for many but not all, on the precipice of great change,

---

* Jonathan Goldberg and Madhavi Menon, "Queering History," *PMLA* 120, no. 5 (Oct. 2005): 1608–1617.

divided between progressive humanism and a desire to embrace conservative, faith-based ideals—bears a remarkable resemblance to our own world.

"I'm interested in the ways in which very old stories can play upon the contemporary condition," Tannahill says. Questions that he asks in the play that link fifteenth century Florence to the twenty-first century include: Why have pleasure and sexuality been so readily scapegoated for political ends in both of these eras? How does a seemingly progressive, liberal society allow a demagogue to rise to power? What is the artist's obligation to their community versus their art? If called to sacrifice, which is of greater value—our art or our people?

Tannahill's own path as an artist has been one of questioning the status quo and often working outside of the box of traditional theatre. Between 2008 and 2016 he wrote and directed plays with his own Toronto-based theatre company, Suburban Beast, which staged work in theatres, galleries, found spaces, and in collaboration with non-professional theatre performers, including night-shift workers and pre-teenagers. From 2012 to 2016 he ran the alternative art space Videofag out of his own home in Toronto, which became one of the city's most influential places for avant-garde and queer theatre. His 2015 book *Theatre of the Unimpressed* is a cri de cœur for a theatre in service to the transformative live event, predicated on artistic risk and unafraid of the possibility of failure.

Like its author, *Botticelli in the Fire* lives outside the norm of the traditional. Neither historical nor contemporary, the play lives across time, asking age-old questions of sexuality, politics, class, and love, which will continue to vex artists and their audiences long into the next millennium.

Kirsten Bowen is Literary Director for Woolly Mammoth Theatre Company in Washington, DC, where she has served as Production Dramaturg on multiple world and DC premieres, including Jordan Tannahill's *Botticelli in the Fire*. Prior to joining Woolly, she was Associate Literary Director for New York's Signature Theatre. She has worked as a dramaturg for the National New Play Network/Kennedy Center's MFA Playwrights' Workshop, Columbia University's School of the Arts, Williamstown Theatre Festival, and American Repertory Theater. She has a B.A. from Smith College and an M.F.A. in Dramaturgy from the ART/MXAT Institute at Harvard University.

Botticelli in the Fire premiered at Canadian Stage's Berkeley Street Theatre, Toronto, in rep with *Sunday in Sodom*, between April 26 and May 15, 2016, with the following cast and creative team:

Sandro Botticelli: Salvatore Antonio
Clarice Orsini: Nicola Correia-Damude
Lorenzo de' Medici: Christopher Morris
Girolamo Savonarola: Alon Nashman
Madre Maria: Valerie Buhagiar
Leonardo da Vinci: Stephen Jackman-Torkoff

Director: Matjash Mrozewski
Set and Costume Designer: James Lavoie
Lighting Designer: Steve Lucas
Composer and Sound Designer: Samuel Sholdice
Projection Consultant: Cameron Davis
Fight Director: Simon Fon
Stage Manager: Michael Sinclair
Assistant Stage Manager: Andrea Baggs
Associate Technical Director: Bryan Steele
Props Builder: Vanessa Janiszewski
Carpenter: Peter Velocci
Production Assistant: Melanie Hall
Head of Wardrobe: Ming Wong

The play was first produced, in its final two-act version, by Woolly Mammoth Theatre in Washington, DC, from May 28 to June 24, 2018, with the following cast and creative team:

Sandro Botticelli: Jon Hudson Odom
Clarice Orsini: Alyssa Wilmoth-Keegan
Lorenzo de' Medici: Cody Nickell
Poggio di Chullu: Earl T. Kim
Girolamo Savonarola: Craig Wallace
Madre Maria: Dawn Ursula
Leonardo da Vinci: James Crichton

Director: Marti Lyons
Set Designer: Misha Kachman
Costume Designer: Ivania Stack
Lighting Designer: Colin K. Bills
Composer and Sound Designer: Christian Frederickson
Production Dramaturg: Kirsten Bowen
Fight Choreographer: Robb Hunter
Intimacy Coach: Lorraine Ressegger-Slone
Production Stage Manager: Rachael Danielle Albert
Assistant Director: Robyn Rikoon
Assistant Stage Manager: Leigh Robinette

CHARACTERS

Sandro Botticelli, an art star in his thirties
Clarice Orsini, a rich and powerful woman in her thirties
Lorenzo de' Medici, a rich and powerful man in his early forties
Poggio di Chullu, a painter and bon vivant in his thirties
Girolamo Savonarola, a charismatic friar in his sixties
Madre Maria, a woman in her fifties
Leonardo da Vinci, a painter in his early twenties

ACT I

I

A spotlight on SANDRO *Botticelli entering the audience from the stage door. He holds an open bottle of wine.*

SANDRO
Do you know what—
Sorry just before we start the show
Do you know what they just asked me in the green room?
If I'd stick around after the show to sign calendars in the lobby
A calendar of my paintings
Uh—no fucking way
Sorry
Proceeds go to some sick actors' fund or something
Uh sorry *no*

 He takes a swig of wine.

Oh, and turn off your fucking cellphones
Alright?
Go on
Take them out
This is real, I'll wait
This has been five hundred years in the making
If I hear a ding I'll kill you
I'm serious

I was talking with a friend the other day and he said:
"don't you think performing a play about yourself is a bit of a vanity project?"
And I was like: 1) this is not just a play it's an *extravaganza*
and 2) vanity?
If you had an eternity to tell yourself the same story over and over
to pick apart every mistake
eventually you'd want an audience too
Because where do you go from here?
Where does it end?
Another five hundred years, over and over—no
No
It stops tonight
Vanity project
Fuck you very much

And I promise you this isn't going to be another tortured fag-artist sob story
Okay maybe it is—sue me
But seriously, it's more of a downfall story
And we all like a good downfall, don't we?
Especially when you're the King Shit
And I was, for a time

State dinners
Commissions
They called me a wunderkind
They called me the poster child of my generation
I painted the fucking Sistine Chapel
Not the ceiling, mind you
just the floor-level frescoes—but still

> *In pools of light* CLARICE *Orsini,* LORENZO *de' Medici, Girolamo* SAVON-
> AROLA, POGGIO *Di Chullu, and Madre* MARIA *appear, singing a choral
> overture, which continues under the following text.*

CLARICE
The thing you gotta know about Botticelli is he had a huge . . . talent
Definitely the biggest I'd ever seen
And he knew how to use it
Other men—they always know when a guy's got a huge talent
Just the way he carried himself
It made them mad with envy
Botticelli had that swagger
He'd be walking down the street and you'd think to yourself
"goddamn what a great fucking painter he must be"

SANDRO
I was at the Medici's palace three times a week

LORENZO
If Botticelli wasn't at a party, no one would stay—

SANDRO
I was their confidant

LORENZO
—and somehow he managed to be at four or five in one night

CLARICE
He had such a big talent, men and women fainted as he walked past

POGGIO
Oh let's be honest, he was the most voracious bottom in Florence

SAVONAROLA
A man of a thousand lovers they said

MARIA
Even as a baby he was insatiable

SANDRO
Ma

MARIA
Well it's true

CLARICE
He had such a big talent, dogs barked at it and then ran away whimpering

MARIA
As a baby I would catch him fondling himself in his crib

SANDRO
Momma, please / I'd rather you—

MARIA
I didn't know what to do
I asked my husband and he just laughed and shrugged
I asked my mother and she told me to say fifty—

CHORUS
—Hail Mary full of grace!

SANDRO
When she asked our priest

MARIA
Father, what do I do with Sandro; he won't stop touching himself
He said, "Bring him back in seven years and I'll take care of it myself"

The CHORUS laughs.

I'm joking
The priest said:

SANDRO
"Tie his hands to the bars of the crib"

MARIA
So that's what I did
I tied his hands to the bars

POGGIO
Well that explains a few of your predilections

SANDRO
The point I was trying to make was—

SAVONAROLA
The tabloids loved him of course

SANDRO
There was a time / when I was—

SAVONAROLA
He was absolutely

SANDRO
—ubiquitous

POGGIO
Girl was fierce

SAVONAROLA
And his depravity—

SANDRO
People would come up to me at a party
and they'd be just dripping with jealousy
I remember this one queen, he said to me
"I heard you once had an orgy with thirty people that lasted a whole weekend"

AndIwaslike: "Once?"
Please
Do your research, girl
Do. Your. Research.
Once
Cute

POGGIO
The truth is—

SANDRO
I was a dog
A dog doesn't understand moderation
A dog eats till it pukes
And when I was living I was *living*
I was eating the marrow from the fucking bone

POGGIO
But in those days—

SANDRO
Everyone was dying young and beautiful
and I thought well fuck if that's the case then

POGGIO
No limits, girl

SANDRO
I wanted to live so badly it was like a madness
'Cause I knew there wasn't anything after

    He gestures around.

Just the fucking void
I was so fucking terrified of the void
But y'all are, don't think I don't know

Everyone was back then too
Scared shitless
They prayed and prayed and prayed—bless
Me?
I was going to wring every last drop outta life while I could

Lights shift.

LEONARDO appears beside SANDRO, standing in his Renaissance finery.

LEONARDO
You look like you crawled out of a back alley

SANDRO
Leo

LEONARDO
This is your gala, Sandro
People've travelled from across the / country to celebrate you—

SANDRO
I know, I know, I—

LEONARDO
—can't show up to the Medici's palace looking like you've been doing lines
   of coke off a toilet seat

SANDRO
I'm sorry

LEONARDO
Here

LEONARDO begins to undress.

SANDRO
What're you doing?

LEONARDO
Put this on

> *LEONARDO hands SANDRO his tunic and jacket. SANDRO hands him his soiled shirt.*

SANDRO
Oh, and did you remember—?

LEONARDO
Yes yes

> *LEONARDO hands SANDRO a stylized carnival plague doctor's mask.*

SANDRO
Ugh why do I have to be the plague doctor?

LEONARDO
Because you're the one with the big nose

SANDRO
It just feels in bad taste

LEONARDO
Exactly, it's perfect for you

> *LEONARDO hands SANDRO the mask.*

> *SANDRO takes LEONARDO's face in his hands and looks into his eyes.*

SANDRO
You're lucky you're so cute

POGGIO appears beside them wearing a half-mask and holding two glasses of champagne.

POGGIO
Well about fucking time
I was starting to think you were going to blow off your own party

POGGIO hands SANDRO one of the champagne flutes.

SANDRO
Oh my god bless you

SANDRO downs the drink as POGGIO lifts his mask to size up LEONARDO.

POGGIO
And speaking of blowing off, this must be the new apprentice

SANDRO
Leo, this is Poggio di Chullu

POGGIO
I've heard so much about you

SANDRO
(to LEONARDO) We apprenticed together back in the day

POGGIO
I taught this fucker everything he knows

SANDRO
Please, if you taught me everything I know you'd be arrested

POGGIO
Little word of advice, sweetie: don't fall in love with him
All his new apprentices do and it breaks my heart

LEONARDO

Thanks, I'll take it under advisement

SANDRO

My god look at the turnout

POGGIO

Frankly I'm surprised anyone came at all

SANDRO

Well fuck you very much

POGGIO

Because of the protests

SANDRO

Ugh, I mean leave those shopfronts alone, amIright?

POGGIO

Listen, if I wasn't here with you tonight I'd be out there too
People are poor, we're living in shitholes, and we're getting sick

SANDRO

And smashing things is not helping

POGGIO

Well the Medici sure the hell aren't either

SANDRO

They have a lot on their plate

LEONARDO

Yeah while everyone else is starving

POGGIO

Sing it

Lights shift. A masquerade party. SANDRO turns to the audience.

SANDRO
(to audience) There were hundreds of people in the ballroom
everyone peering in my direction but too shy to approach
So the three of us were this little island in a sea of fawning acolytes
until all of a sudden a hush fell over the crowd and from across the room—

LORENZO and CLARICE appear in their royal regalia, wearing golden masks.

POGGIO
My god there they are
(to LEONARDO) Lorenzo the Magnificent and his wife Clarice Orsini

SANDRO
Do you reckon that's real gold?

POGGIO
Girl, there's two giraffes in the back garden
Yes, that's real gold

LORENZO lifts his mask to address the gala.

LORENZO
Ladies and gentlemen
it's my great pleasure to welcome you all here this evening

SANDRO
(to LEONARDO) How do I look?

LEONARDO
Roguish

LORENZO
We are in the midst of a rebirth
A rebirth in the ideals of art and science that once brought greatness to
    our ancient brothers
And in these trying times it is the arts in particular
which give us an opportunity to consider that which lifts us
that which unites us
and that which makes us human
We are here tonight to celebrate a man who
through his divine gift
reflects back to us our humanity

POGGIO
(murmuring to LEONARDO) Let's be honest, we're here because of the open bar

LORENZO
A man who masterpiece by masterpiece
is pulling us by the balls out of the dark ages and into the light
Into a world built on the bedrock of reason and fact
not the shifting sands of ignorance and fear
Tonight we honour a man I am proud to also call a close friend

POGGIO
(murmuring to SANDRO) He can afford to buy as many friends as he wants

SANDRO
And don't you wish you were one of them?

POGGIO
Friends come and go, babe
enemies accumulate

LORENZO
It gives me immense pleasure tonight to bestow the Order of San Marco
on none other than Sandro Botticelli

Lights shift. The gala falls away. SANDRO *is once more by himself.*

SANDRO
The crowd erupted and parted for me like the Red Sea
as a hundred white balloons fell from the ceiling
and after Lorenzo pinned the medallion to my chest and shook my hand
I shook hands with Clarice
and as we did something passed between us
our eyes lingering a second too long
She found me by myself on the balcony later that night

Spot appears on CLARICE'*s face; she is standing right beside* SANDRO.

CLARICE
If I have to make any more small talk I'm going to smash this glass and cut
someone's throat

SANDRO
Well I
hope I don't disappoint

CLARICE *searches for her lighter.* SANDRO *offers her a light.*

CLARICE
That's convenient

Beat. She smokes.

When people down there see pictures of tonight
all of us dressed up like this, toasting your brilliance
what do you think goes through their minds?

SANDRO
What . . . a bunch of fucking assholes

CLARICE
And do you know what my husband thinks they're thinking?

SANDRO shakes his head.

Wow
The Medici are pulling us by the balls out of the Dark Ages

SANDRO
Right

CLARICE
The streets are burning

SANDRO
People are—

CLARICE
—furious, of course they are, wouldn't you be?
The plague is back
There are bodies rotting in the streets

SANDRO
(to audience) I couldn't believe she was speaking so candidly
And then, as if catching herself—

CLARICE
I don't know why I'm saying this to you

SANDRO
What do you think should be done then?
To stop the plague

Beat.

CLARICE
Would you believe
that's
the first time anyone's asked me that

LORENZO
(calling from off stage) Clarice!

CLARICE
I'm sorry
You know how possessive he can be

SANDRO
I want to hear your ideas

CLARICE
Well I'm afraid that'll have to wait for one of our sessions

LORENZO
(calling from off stage) Clarice!

SANDRO
Sorry, one of our—?

CLARICE
Did Lorenzo not mention the commission?

SANDRO
Uh . . . no

CLARICE
Oh
Well it just so happens the award comes with a big commission

She finishes her cigarette and flicks it away.

To paint me

Blackout.

I I

The sounds of intense orgasms fill the space.

A large canvas is on an easel in the middle of the room, below which are sprawled the naked bodies of SANDRO and CLARICE. SANDRO's face is buried below the sheets and CLARICE screams in ecstasy. He is eating her out, and doing a great job of it.

After a moment SANDRO pops his head up from under the sheets to catch his breath.

SANDRO
Maybe we should—

CLARICE
I swear to god if you stop—

SANDRO dives back under the bedsheets and CLARICE moans with renewed vigour.

LEONARDO enters the room with a handful of mail, notices the amorous pair, and exits unseen.

CLARICE climaxes thunderously.

SANDRO pops his head back out from under the sheets.

SANDRO
For the record, when I suggested we eat out, I meant breakfast

CLARICE
Was I too rough?

Adjusting his jaw:

SANDRO
No I'm good

CLARICE runs her hand through SANDRO's hair.

CLARICE
Hey

SANDRO
Hey

CLARICE
That was nice

SANDRO
Mmm

They kiss.

CLARICE
What time is it?

SANDRO looks for his phone.

SANDRO
Where's my—?
Ugh . . . it's too far

CLARICE
Your little butt boy will be here any minute

SANDRO
I wish you'd stop calling him that
Especially to his face

> *CLARICE rises.*

CLARICE
I should wash up

SANDRO
We really can't do this every morning

CLARICE
Why?
Because of Lorenzo?
I've told you, we barely sleep in the same palace anymore

SANDRO
I just—

CLARICE
It's fine

> *CLARICE walks off stage.*

(calling) In case you haven't noticed, there are other things on his mind

> *SANDRO flops back into the sheets and begins jerking off.*

> *LEONARDO enters.*

LEONARDO
Morrrrning

SANDRO immediately desists masturbating and acts nonchalant.

SANDRO
You're early

LEONARDO
The new horse-hair fine-tips arrived in the mail

SANDRO
Fabulous

Looking through mail:

LEONARDO
Would you like to make a donation to help repatriate the relics of / St. Peter back to the—

SANDRO
No

LEONARDO
The rest are bills

SANDRO
Put them on the table, I'll deal with it

LEONARDO
Are you visiting your mother today?

SANDRO
Fuck is it already Sunday?

LEONARDO
Seems like your hands are a little full

SANDRO
That's two weeks in a row, that's so bad
I just—

    SANDRO glances at the canvas and stops.

Jesus Christ

LEONARDO
What?
Oh I stayed late to fix the feet last night
I know they were giving you some trouble

SANDRO
Uh huh

LEONARDO
It's just a—fix

SANDRO
Right

LEONARDO
If you—

SANDRO
I was going to deal with them today

LEONARDO
I know
I just—

    SANDRO nods. Pause.

I can change them back if you don't—
you know

Pause.

SANDRO
Leo, can I ask you something?

LEONARDO nods.

How did you do this?

Pause.

I mean this—

SANDRO imitates the pose of Venus's right foot.

How her foot feels rooted now as if it's really—

He gestures.

The shading here

He points.

LEONARDO
I don't know, I just—

SANDRO
It's good
It's very good

LEONARDO registers the compliment for a moment.

LEONARDO
Well if you don't mind me making another suggestion
Zephyr right now?
We don't get any sense that he's connected to Venus's movement or the waves

I mean it doesn't even look like he's blowing
For all we know he's about to you know *(mimes vomiting)* puke or something
So my suggestion, and I know this sounds a bit literal
but a few little wisps of breath
a few dashes of white / right here could really—

SANDRO
Right, well why don't we—

LEONARDO
Look

> *LEONARDO takes up the paint pallet.*

SANDRO
Heyheyhey

LEONARDO
Just—

> *LEONARDO applies a few brisk dashes of white to the canvas. He stands back and both he and SANDRO consider the results.*

SANDRO
(impressed) Okay

LEONARDO
See?
Now it's—
It connects it, right?
We get a sense that he's—

SANDRO
He's the wind

LEONARDO
Right
And speaking of which, do you mind if I open a window?

Still processing LEONARDO's *intervention in the painting:*

SANDRO
What?

LEONARDO
It's just a little musty in here

SANDRO
No, no, no the protests disturb Clarice

LEONARDO
Uh huh

SANDRO
We—

LEONARDO
Her cum is still on your face by the way

SANDRO wipes his mouth.

SANDRO
We were just—

LEONARDO
I know

SANDRO
She runs this city
She could have me thrown in prison

LEONARDO
How romantic

They hear the shower turning on.

You know, Venus—I've been thinking
how appropriate really
Goddess of beauty, yes, but also perpetually dissatisfied
Always desiring something greater for herself
Married to Vulcan, a powerful god, sure
but also a dull metal worker, totally banal
No sex, no fun, no interesting conversations
So Venus goes looking / for better company elsewhere—

SANDRO
Leo

LEONARDO
—and finds the delectable Mars and naturally they start fucking until—

SANDRO
She's a means to an end

LEONARDO
Is everyone?

SANDRO
Are you being a little grumpy bitch this morning?

LEONARDO
There were two bodies at the end of the street this morning covered in bedsheets
No one will touch them or go near them—

SANDRO
Listen—

LEONARDO
—and it's like you're pretending not to notice

SANDRO
What do you think I'm doing here?
With her? With this painting?
When the plague comes I'm going to need / friends in high places
With influence

LEONARDO
The plague is already here, it's on our doorstep

SANDRO
The best doctors, the best medicine
How do you think I'm going to get that?

LEONARDO
Well I'm glad you've worked it all out

SANDRO
Sweetie: listen to me
We are modern people
This is the fucking Renaissance
The earth is round
The earth goes around the sun
We're not going to die of the plague

LEONARDO
Because the Medici will—

SANDRO
—pull me favours, yes

LEONARDO
You're fucking his wife

SANDRO
Sometimes I wonder if they like—

LEONARDO
What?

SANDRO
Like maybe they have some kind of arrangement

LEONARDO
Wait, you think he *knows* that you're / fucking his wife

>   *SANDRO takes out his phone.*

SANDRO
Look at this text he sent me last weekend

>   *LEONARDO reads the text.*

LEONARDO
Huh

SANDRO
"How's the painting cumming along?"
"Coming" spelt with a "u"

LEONARDO
Could be an autocorrect

SANDRO
Right

LEONARDO
Or a typo
I mean the u and the o are very close on the keypad

SANDRO
Listen, I've been around long enough to know:
the elites are all perverts
They have their little games
and if you can play by their rules they'll take care of you
And when the shit goes down, we're going to need their—

> *CLARICE walks out of the bathroom holding a large white towel.*

CLARICE
Sandro, did you steal these towels from the palace?

> *CLARICE notices LEONARDO and wraps herself up in the towel, suddenly more self-conscious.*

SANDRO
Ha, funny you should mention that—

CLARICE
Do you think it's a bit much?
I suddenly had this doubt in the shower about the pose
That maybe it's all a little—

SANDRO
Much

CLARICE
Debauched

SANDRO
Clarice, hi, I'm Botticelli, debauched is what I do
If your husband wanted you in a nun's habit he should have commissioned
 Fra Filippo

CLARICE
But is it in good taste?
I mean it's just—such a departure

SANDRO
From good taste?

CLARICE
From everything else, you know, out there

SANDRO
Precisely, why should I just add another canvas to the heap
of "everything else out there"?

CLARICE
He doesn't know it's a nude

SANDRO
He must

CLARICE
I don't think so

SANDRO
Just tell him a painter can't ignore inspiration

CLARICE
I think he was hoping to put this in the dining room though

SANDRO
Clarice, enough, you're stressing me out
(to LEONARDO) Put on my Chill Out playlist, will you?

LEONARDO exits.

CLARICE
I prefer our sessions when we're alone

SANDRO
Yes, but those are terribly unproductive

CLARICE
Besides, I can tell he hates me

SANDRO
Don't be ridiculous

CLARICE
Was he another hustler you pulled off the street?

SANDRO
No no he's the bastard son of a farm girl from Vinci

CLARICE
Well I don't trust him

SANDRO
Leonardo?
He's been with me three months

CLARICE
There's just something about him
Still, fabulous bone structure, don't you think?
You could cut an apple with his jaw

SANDRO
Honestly? He's the real fucking deal
It took him three hours to learn how to mix tempera with egg yolk
It took me three months
A couple mornings ago I came in here and he'd fixed your mouth
I couldn't even tell what he'd done but it was suddenly perfect

I sketched an angel and he corrected my proportions
The length of her arm, the distance between her collarbone and waist
He doesn't even realize how brilliant he is

    SANDRO crosses to the easel and begins getting ready to work.

CLARICE
You have a little crush

SANDRO
Please

CLARICE
You do, look at you
I haven't seen you like this before
All earnest

SANDRO
No no he's just a little—puppy dog tugging on his leash
woof woof, you know

CLARICE
God that makes me—

SANDRO
What?

CLARICE
The way you look at him

SANDRO
Come here

    They kiss. Music begins to play.

CLARICE
Which reminds me
this morning Lorenzo was saying how much he misses your squash games

SANDRO
Did he?
How sweet

CLARICE
I was supposed to tell you
he wants to see you on the court tomorrow at ten a.m.

> *LEONARDO returns and begins mixing paint while observing the other two.*

SANDRO
What?

CLARICE
Just bring your runners, he has rackets

> *SANDRO glances towards LEONARDO (and does so periodically throughout the rest of the scene).*

SANDRO
I have—brunch plans

CLARICE
Well you'll just have to cancel them
He'll send along a driver at quarter-to

SANDRO
You've been here for two hours and / you tell me now

CLARICE
I didn't want to spoil the mood

SANDRO
Are you fucking with me?

CLARICE
Excuse me?

SANDRO
Yes you are, look at you fucking with me

CLARICE
No I am / not fucking with you

SANDRO
Do the two of you—?

CLARICE
What?

SANDRO
Does he know?

CLARICE
No
Why are you even—?
Have you said / something?

SANDRO
Of course I haven't

CLARICE
'Cause I'd have your tongue cut out

SANDRO
Then—?

CLARICE

Do you have any idea how much he talks about you?
You quiet his mind, Sandro

SANDRO

We have—a special connection

CLARICE

And he's anxious to see the canvas

SANDRO

Anxious?

CLARICE

Yes, but I told him / he'd just have to wait

SANDRO

I just want to make sure we're all on the same page

CLARICE

There's only one page to be on

SANDRO

Well, thank you for the invitation
You can tell him—

CLARICE

You can just tell him: you were inspired

CLARICE *resumes her pose.*

Oh and do me a favour
Stop looking at the boy

Lights shift.

I I I

A spotlight appears on SANDRO. *He speaks to the audience. The* CHORUS
sing faintly, in halting soprano.

SANDRO
I know what you're thinking: shit girl
Watch yourself
Yes   **CHORUS**
Oh yes   one-tenth
These were dangerous times   is a quarter
And if you wanted to survive, not just survive   below the knee
but maybe even thrive a little, if you could be so lucky   to the root
you had to play a lot of sides, alright   one-tenth
you had to play so many sides   eyes
you didn't even know what game you were playing anymore   knee

*In the upstage shadows cloaked figures in plague doctor masks carry
bodies one by one and pile them as if in a mass grave.*

And Leo was right   breasts
The plague was back
I remember years ago when I was a kid—   one-eighth
                                                             one-sixth
Lights up faintly on MARIA.   is a quarter

MARIA   below the foot
My goodness, my little Sandro had nightmares   to the root
Nightmares all the time   of a man
He'd wake up in the middle of the night screaming and crying
and he'd run into my room   eyes
tears streaming down his face
"Sweetie, what's wrong?"   knee
In his dreams he told me he saw his skin peeling off his body
I held him, I rocked him   breasts

Of course he had seen the images on TV
The plague, the piles of bodies in the streets   one-tenth
"Sweetie, you don't have to worry   is a quarter
You're not going to get the plague"   is
"Why?" he'd ask
"Because only sinners get the plague   eyes
And you—your soul is like a cloud   knee
White and incorruptible
Beyond the reach of the hands of men"   breasts
I remember one night, to get him to stop crying
I took him into the kitchen and made him a peanut butter sandwich
because I knew that was his favourite
I remember I stepped out for a moment to use the toilet
and when I returned
I saw Sandro take the knife out of the peanut butter and lick it like this

     MARIA and SANDRO demonstrate licking peanut butter off a knife.

Down one side
and then down the other
so slowly
savouring the taste
eyes closed
lost in it
letting nothing go to waste
He didn't know I saw him
But I did, from the doorway of the kitchen
It was only an instant
But in that moment I saw
how bottomless his pleasure was
And it terrified me

     Lights shift. The plague doctors continue to drag and pile bodies in
     the background.

SANDRO
At night Poggio and I would hit the town hard
and I mean can't-find-your-way-home-don't-remember-your-name hard
And one morning, a couple months before the gala
the sun was coming up, people were just beginning to open their shops
when all of a sudden across the street—

> *Lights rise faintly on* SAVONAROLA. *He is speaking into a microphone*
> *attached to a portable amp.*

SAVONAROLA
Fleas
Let me tell you about fleas
Fleas feast on the blood of others
Fleas feast on the blood, sweat, and tears of others
sucking money from the Church and the people
to fill their homes with gold and jewels and blasphemous art as the people starve

SANDRO
This like ridiculous street preacher foaming at the mouth

SAVONAROLA
These fleas we call the Medici
and the artists and opportunists who get fat off the Medici
Let me tell you about fleas
Fleas spread the plague

POGGIO
Whatdoeshethink, this is some small town in the south?

SAVONAROLA
The city is sick with the pestilence of sin
And like Sodom and Gomorrah, its day of reckoning is near

> POGGIO *laughs.*

POGGIO
Sodom and—

SANDRO
I pitied him really

POGGIO
You've got to be kidding

SANDRO
People are educated here
They talk to god, if at all, quietly and privately

SAVONAROLA
Brothers and sisters, we have all been distracted!

SANDRO
This was one of the most progressive cities in the world

SAVONAROLA
In this age of darkness we have been distracted from the one thing that
    truly matters
and that is our soul
That is the one thing the plague cannot touch
And to the fleas that suck our blood
We will pinch them off one by one
We will burn them with matches
We will be the hailstorm that breaks the heads of those / who do not take shelter

   POGGIO *lunges and grabs* SAVONAROLA's *microphone.*

POGGIO
Honey, this is the worst karaoke song I've ever heard in my life
Why don't you try / "girls just wanna have fun" *(continues singing)*

SAVONAROLA
Get your—let—get off of me

> *Lights fade on* POGGIO *as he and* SAVONAROLA *wrestle over the microphone,* POGGIO *singing Cyndi Lauper's "Girls Just Want to Have Fun."*

SANDRO
It's amazing how much can change in a few months

I V

> *Lights rise on the set of a television news talk show.*

> *The* HOST *(played by the same actor who plays* LORENZO*) sits in an armchair across from* SAVONAROLA. *The interview is filmed via live-feed camera and projected on the massive wall behind them. We cut in on the interview mid-flow.*

HOST
But seriously, here you are, the year's big overnight success story—

SAVONAROLA
You know, I, I keep hearing this and I'm—

> SAVONAROLA *chuckles.*

Listen, I'm in my sixties
I've been working at this a long time
This doesn't just happen overnight

HOST
But you have to admit it's been a hell of a few months

SAVONAROLA
Well—

HOST
A bestselling book, huge turnouts at your sermons—

SAVONAROLA
Right, but this is not about me
This is what the press and the Medici don't seem to understand
This is about returning power to the people from a corrupt elite
that is profoundly out of touch with their lives
and profoundly out of touch with God

HOST
Sure but—

SAVONAROLA
The Medici are bankers!

SAVONAROLA chuckles.

They're just a family of usurers, they're not kings, they're not gods
But we've let them think they are
And now they're treating the city like their personal wallet

HOST
But this isn't really about corruption for you, is it?

SAVONAROLA
Well—

HOST
In terms of—

SAVONAROLA
Well it is about corruption, of course it is
The deepest kind of corruption
Why do you think the Lord sent this plague?

> *Beat.*

HOST
Are you—?

SAVONAROLA
I'm asking you, yes

HOST
I—

> *The* HOST *lifts his hands as if to say "Who am I to answer that question?"*

SAVONAROLA
The Medici are trying to put Man, put *themselves* at the centre of the universe
and we're saying no
No to their pagan gods and golden idols made by their sodomite artists
Sodomites who are celebrated and walking the streets
not even making an attempt to hide what they are

HOST
You seem to be particularly / preoccupied with—

SAVONAROLA
Have you been, sorry to interrupt, but have you been to the countryside lately?
I'm from the countryside
Do you know what people's nickname for Florence is there?

HOST
I can imagine

SAVONAROLA
God is unequivocal, in fact there are few things He is so unequivocal about
   as sodomites
Frankly, we're lucky all He's sent us is the plague

HOST
What would you say to the people—
Because there were a lot of people upset with the Medici before you came along

SAVONAROLA
Sure

HOST
So what would you say to those who might say
okay well I hate the Medici, they're corrupt, the plague is back
they're not doing anything
but this Savonarola guy is just too—

SAVONAROLA
Extreme

HOST
Way too extreme for me
Calling for children to spy on their parents
For sex workers to be chastised
for the streets to be policed for indecent dress
A hotline for neighbours to report on their neighbours

SAVONAROLA
Wake up
That's what I say to them
This is a war for people's souls
And you're either standing with God or you're standing in His way

The image cuts to static. Sounds of protests in the darkness.

V

Lights up on SANDRO's *studio.*

SANDRO, POGGIO, *and* LEONARDO *stagger through the door.*

The canvas is turned away from the audience, covered in a tarp.

POGGIO
And I looked him in the eye and I said, "Sweetie, you better drop that knife
'Cause I refuse to be killed by someone wearing taffeta sleeves"

SANDRO
You've got to draw the line somewhere

POGGIO
Slashes and puffed no less

SANDRQ *runs his thumb along a gash on* LEONARDO's *forehead.*

SANDRO
It'll probably leave a scar

LEONARDO
Shit, really?

POGGIO
You're too pretty anyway, it's disgusting

SANDRO
We just gotta accept you guys can't be seen walking around with me anymore
It's too dangerous

SANDRO *grabs a cloth and some rubbing alcohol from his workbench.*

Over the following lines SANDRO *sits* LEONARDO *down and administers the alcohol to his wound.*

POGGIO
Honey, we were all there screaming with our wine spritzers
We were not exactly being discrete, 'specially not Angelo

SANDRO
Plus, I probably shouldn't have flashed my dick at them

POGGIO laughs.

POGGIO
No you shouldn't have

SANDRO
But let's be honest, that's what all those assholes secretly want anyway

POGGIO
You know the fucked-up thing is I recognized two of those guys
They were there with me at the first protests
I was there at the first fucking one handing out bottles of water
and now they're throwing a wine spritzer in my face
I have to walk an extra five blocks home now just to avoid the protests

SANDRO
The walking will do you good, girl

POGGIO
I stood shoulder to shoulder with those people
and now he's turned them into I don't know what
Some crazed fuckin' god mob

LEONARDO
What was that word they started shouting at us?

POGGIO
Faggots

LEONARDO
What does that even mean?

POGGIO
Bundles of wood

LEONARDO
I'm sorry?

SANDRO
Bundles of—?

POGGIO
Faggots are kindling

> *Silence.*

SANDRO
Lorenzo's losing his grip of the city

> *POGGIO mimes a hand job.*

POGGIO
Funny, I thought you'd be helping him with his grip

LEONARDO
Oh no his hands are full with another Medici

POGGIO
Oh I am literally dying of curiosity

SANDRO
And I'll be literally dead if you gossip about it

POGGIO
Honey, give me some credit, I know what's off limits

SANDRO
Well it's off limits
I have to play fucking squash with him in the morning

POGGIO
Well la-di-dah

SANDRO
Right

POGGIO
Is she naked?

SANDRO turns and looks at him.

I heard you're painting her starkers

SANDRO
Who told you that?

POGGIO
Holy fuck she is!

SANDRO
I'm neither confirming nor denying

POGGIO
Are you insane?
People are going to lose their minds

SANDRO
They'll be too busy trying to pick their jaws off the ground

POGGIO
It's good?

SANDRO
Oh it's good

POGGIO
Really though?

SANDRO
Maybe the best

POGGIO
Oh, honey, you gotta show me the receipts if you're going to say shit like that

POGGIO *makes to get up.*

SANDRO
Sit your ass down

POGGIO
You're kidding

SANDRO
Not until it's finished

POGGIO
Your best?

SANDRO
No
I mean the best ever

POGGIO
Oh that's sadistic

SANDRO
You'll make a bunch of snipey comments—

POGGIO
I won't!

SANDRO
—and it'll mess me up

POGGIO
And after all the help I gave you with the *Primavera*!

SANDRO
Please, when you saw it I had one figure left

POGGIO
And I was the one who told you you should model him off Leo!

SANDRO
Oh wow I should give you half my commission

POGGIO
And now—yeah maybe you should
because now all everyone talks about is how fuckable Mercury turned out!

SANDRO
I'm not showing you the canvas
Besides it'd be a breach of trust

POGGIO
Oh please, you're painting her completely naked / what's left to be breached?

SANDRO
I'm a man of honour

POGGIO
Hold on hold on, what are we talking about here, are we talking—

POGGIO makes a gesture for "breasts." SANDRO is coy. POGGIO makes a gesture for "vagina" and SANDRO smiles.

No

SANDRO
Well

POGGIO
Is it red?

SANDRO makes an exasperated gesture.

Oh don't think the entire city isn't wondering about those carpet and drapes!

POGGIO jumps up and begins rushing towards the canvas. SANDRO jumps up and grabs him. They tumble to the ground howling with laugher.

Oooo I'm hurt

SANDRO
Shit, did I fall on you?

POGGIO
No, Sandro, I'm your best friend
This is the biggest commission of your life, your whole life
and you won't even share it with me
not even a tiny little infinitesimal little fart of a peek

SANDRO
You're a little fart

POGGIO
It hurts me

SANDRO
A little queef, a little queer queef

POGGIO
I can't believe they trust you with royalty
You're a man child

> *POGGIO suddenly palms a palette of paint and smears it across SANDRO's face, distracting him, and dashes to the canvas. POGGIO rips the tarp off the canvas and gasps. The painting remains turned away from the audience.*

Ave, o Maria, piena di grazia

SANDRO
It's not finished

POGGIO
They're going to kill you
They're going to worship you
don't get me wrong
But they are going to kill you

> *LEONARDO walks over and points to the painting.*

LEONARDO
What do you think about the angle of her leg here?
Does something seem off about it?

> *POGGIO bursts out laughing. He turns to SANDRO and points at the painting.*

POGGIO
I really can't believe this
I mean nobody has done this since the Romans

LEONARDO
Not even

POGGIO
Sorry?

LEONARDO
Not even the Romans painted a nude of this scale before

POGGIO
Seriously, are you trying to martyr yourself?
Do you realize—I mean it's fucking brilliant, don't get me wrong
but you do realize how many people this is going to piss off, right?

SANDRO
Are you not moved?

POGGIO
Of course I am!
That's not the point!
Are you ready for the shitstorm?

SANDRO
When it's finished—

POGGIO
Sandro

SANDRO
—there'll be no denying its beauty

POGGIO
There's no denying it now
But beauty's not enough

    SANDRO covers the canvas with the tarp once more.

SANDRO
You see what I mean?

POGGIO
What?

SANDRO
You piss on whatever I'm working on

POGGIO
C'mon, that's not what I was—

SANDRO
You do, you have no idea no fucking idea how, how delicate
how specific the alchemy of this is and how
you / you just blunder in here and upset everything

POGGIO
You think you can paint the Medici's wife buck / naked and not provoke—?

SANDRO
She is giving me permission to make myself naked with her do you understand she is pushing me inspiring me to unlock something in myself that I
mean you think the Vatican the fucking Church would ever let me—this
this is—ancient—this—

POGGIO
Sandro, I don't want to lose you and that is why I'm sitting here with you
drinking this shitty wine from Vinci that tastes like piss

He turns to LEONARDO.

no offence but I'm a connoisseur and I don't mean of wine
sitting here as we bandage each other up
because who the hell knows when those assholes / will bust in here with—

SANDRO
Stop it

POGGIO
Stop what?
It's already begun, honey
There're people in the piazza shouting "burn the sodomites!"

SANDRO
I know but—

POGGIO
I'll tell you what I know:
they'll start with Verrocchio and his butt boys
and then they'll come for Antonio and my fat ass—

LEONARDO
See?

SANDRO
C'mon

POGGIO
—and then they'll probably round off the cinders with Paulo de Sica—!

SANDRO
Shut up
Okay?
You think this helps?
Filling Leo's head with this bullshit?

POGGIO
And what about your head?
It's so far up the Medici's ass you don't even realize how dark it's gotten out here
Not all of us can be the court fairy

SANDRO
Wow

POGGIO
Yes wow it's dark, alright, it's fucking bleak out there and you
you've got to wake up to it because we all know
The queens tell me you're too much of a big shot now
You've forgotten about us
Too busy fucking around with royalty
and I stick up for you, I stick up for you every time
I don't mind being your poor sissy-ass friend, babe
I don't mind being in your shadow
but do not forget who you are at the end of the day
Do not forget you are a worthless faggot
Just like the rest of us

SANDRO
Christians don't burn people

POGGIO
I'm sorry?

SANDRO
Say what you like about them
their politics, their home decor, their ridiculous children's names
they do not burn people
And you know why?
Because they've been burned
Romans used to burn Christians

POGGIO
Oh please—

SANDRO
Do you know how many of their martyrs were burned on pyres?

POGGIO
Do you think any of those idiots out there in the piazza
is cracking open their codex and reading about Saint Polycarp and Lucia?

SANDRO bursts out laughing. Then POGGIO starts to laugh.

You brilliant idiots, I love you so goddamn much

*LEONARDO refills POGGIO and SANDRO's wine glasses. He hands their
glasses to them.*

LEONARDO
Don't you think it's funny
All those saints were burned for their love of a man
and now they want to burn us for the same thing

SANDRO raises his glass.

SANDRO
Saint Poggio
Patron saint of sucking off married men in city parks

POGGIO
Yes and my holy relic will just be my withered hand giving you the middle finger

They laugh.

Nel nome del Padre e del Figlio e dello Spirito Santo Amen

They all raise their glasses and toast.

SANDRO, LEONARDO, & POGGIO
Gay men!

Lights shift.

V I

A squash court at the Medici Palace. SANDRO and LORENZO are in runners, T-shirts, shorts, and wearing sweatbands around their foreheads. CLARICE sits in a lawn chair to the side, reading a magazine.

LORENZO
We'll hang him

CLARICE
No
No, no, no

LORENZO
Right in the fucking piazza where he preaches

CLARICE
You'll have an uprising
He's baiting you, do you get that?
And you can't bite
You have to give the people a vision

LORENZO
I'm giving them the goddamn Renaissance, what more do they fucking want?

CLARICE
People are scared, they're dying, they—

LORENZO
—want a miracle from the fucking sky and I don't have one

CLARICE
Well I might

LORENZO
Oh really?

CLARICE
Sewers

LORENZO
I'm sorry?

CLARICE
People are dumping their waste into the streets and—

> *LORENZO begins laughing. He looks at SANDRO and SANDRO begins laughing too, unsure if that's the correct response.*

—fleas are breeding there and spreading—why are you laughing?

LORENZO
Savonarola is offering the people god and you want to offer them sewers?

CLARICE
This is the single—

> *LORENZO is still laughing.*

LORENZO
Oh yes I can see it now—Lorenzo the Effluent!
His father built the basilica and he built a tunnel of shit, how inspiring!

> *LORENZO turns to SANDRO.*

You know all this is her fault in the first place

SANDRO
Oh?

CLARICE
I swear to god if you say / that one more time

LORENZO
She begged me to bring him to Florence
She said he's a true prophet

CLARICE
No, I offered him safe haven
It's a city of / free speech

LORENZO
I said fine, I'll indulge her
It was either that or a dachshund
and I've never really been one for small dogs
So we bring him to Florence
Right away he starts acting up
Ranting on the street corners
Blaming Clarice and me for all sorts of horrors, the ungrateful bastard
At first I think nothing of it
This city's full of crazies, / what's another?

CLARICE
He is not / just some crazy

LORENZO
First it's a crowd of eighty or a hundred
A few weeks later it's up to a thousand
His last sermon—if you can call it that
seven thousand people

SANDRO
Are you nervous?

LORENZO
Damn right I'm nervous
He's busting my fucking balls

CLARICE
Well in case you haven't noticed
there's a lot of sick and dying people and they want answers
and they're not happy with the answers Lorenzo has for them

SANDRO
But all this about being the fleas sucking the people's blood—

CLARICE
That's just rhetoric for the masses

SANDRO
Burn the sodomites?

LORENZO
The first time I met him I—

LORENZO laughs.

I was giving him a tour of the San Marco convent
and this nun in a wheelchair coasted past us
and I said to him: "Hey, Father, look: Virgin Mobile"

LORENZO bursts out laughing.

He didn't get it
He has no sense of humour

CLARICE
Well ignore him at your peril
That's what I say

LORENZO
Oh is that what you say?
Thanks for the support, Clarice
I'm not fucking ignoring him

CLARICE
You're dismissing him
He's speaking to people's souls
He's giving them hope and / you're dismissing him—

LORENZO
Fine but he's mostly speaking to the souls of the illiterate and ignorant
I mean let's be honest / that's where most of his base seems to be

    CLARICE stands.

CLARICE
I'm tired of you patronizing me

LORENZO
No one is—

CLARICE
(to SANDRO) Lorenzo can't imagine why anyone would challenge him
He doesn't believe in god but believes he has a / god-given right to power

LORENZO
He and his death cult want to take us back to the fucking Dark Ages

CLARICE
The friar is / speaking for the people
He is giving them hope

LORENZO
Hatred of reason
Hatred of liberty
Hated of sex
Hatred of women
Hatred of pleasure and desire
Hatred of the self, of himself, I bet he does
I bet he hates himself
I sure the hell do

CLARICE
He believes in people's souls

LORENZO
He believes in dominance and submission

CLARICE
Please, you love dominance and submission

> *LORENZO laughs.*

The only thing you believe in is yourself

LORENZO
People have the right to do everything in their power
to achieve the greatest amount of pleasure possible to them
assuming—

> *CLARICE makes to interrupt.*

Assuming
they don't infringe on the right of others to do the same
Simple as that

CLARICE
Oh is it?

LORENZO
Yes

CLARICE
Why don't you tell Mariana that?

LORENZO
Who?

CLARICE
Mariana

LORENZO
Who the fuck / is Mariana?

CLARICE
Our head maid for twelve years
Her son just died of the plague
We gave her flowers this morning

LORENZO
I would
I would tell it to her face

CLARICE
Some people need an afterlife, Lorenzo
because you've made this one unbearable for them

>   *CLARICE storms out.*

LORENZO
It's nothing new, really
My father dealt with the same thing
There's always a plague
There's always a fire
And there's always a friar who wants to throw things in it

LORENZO takes out a hunting knife and cuts off a tag on his sports bag with it.

You following the playoffs?

SANDRO
Not really

　Silence.

LORENZO
The markets?

SANDRO
You mean like—stocks?

LORENZO
They took a nosedive this morning
Everyone's—jumpy

　SANDRO nods.

I trust you won't share that little episode
with your queers at some art party now

SANDRO
No, no

　SANDRO chuckles.

LORENZO
You can be a terrible gossip sometimes

　SANDRO mimes zipping his lips, throwing away the key—a little too eager to please.

LORENZO smiles, slaps SANDRO's back, and nods to the squash court.
SANDRO clearly doesn't want to actually play, but dutifully acquiesces.

The two men play squash.

LORENZO decimates SANDRO.

Between rounds LORENZO grabs his water bottle and shoots water into
his mouth.

Clarice makes me so—I'm not fucking ignoring—
There are a thousand doctors and nurses working round the clock right now
Why do you think we passed that emergency budget?

SANDRO
If the unrest gets worse—

LORENZO
Oh it's going to get worse, trust me
But we'll weather it
We always do

SANDRO
At the villa?

LORENZO looks at SANDRO and bursts out laughing.

LORENZO
You're such a little cunt

SANDRO laughs too, uncertain if this is the correct response.

They resume the game.

We must have you back up there soon
I miss our walks together up there

SANDRO
Me too

LORENZO
We should go to the villa
I've just been so fucking busy
But we should, we should go to the villa
and go for one of our walks together
Nice bottle of wine, laugh around the fire

SANDRO
I would like that

LORENZO
And you can even bring your latest flavour of the month, what's his name?

SANDRO
Leonardo's just my—

LORENZO
That's right, Leonardo
I can't keep track, you're so damn voracious

> LORENZO *wins that round, laughs, and slaps* SANDRO *on the back.*

You're my only friend, you know that?

SANDRO
What?

LORENZO
You must know that

SANDRO
Well I—

LORENZO
You're the only person who doesn't want anything from me, Sandro
Everyone in the world, they just—
they just see what I can do for them
But you—I can be real with you

SANDRO
I feel the same

LORENZO
Which
means more to me these days than ever
As you might imagine

SANDRO
Of course

LORENZO
You uh
didn't reply to my text

SANDRO
Oh?

LORENZO
How's it coming?

SANDRO
The—

LORENZO
—painting

SANDRO
It's great

LORENZO
Twenty sittings!

SANDRO
Yeah

LORENZO
Wow

SANDRO
Yeah

LORENZO
Is that usual?

SANDRO
Well—

LORENZO
What kind of painting requires twenty sittings?

SANDRO
A masterpiece

LORENZO
And is it?

SANDRO
There has never been a painting like it

LORENZO
You've outdone yourself

SANDRO
I . . . didn't hold back
Like you said

LORENZO
I did, didn't I, I said—

SANDRO
—don't hold back, so—

LORENZO
Well then I must come by your studio and take a peek

SANDRO
A peek?

LORENZO
My curiosity is inflamed

SANDRO
It's uh it's still very much in process

LORENZO
Oh of course, I know
I'd just love to see how it's coming along
It's been a rather sizable investment, after all

SANDRO
Right

LORENZO
Not least of which being my wife's time

SANDRO
She's been very—patient with me

LORENZO
I'll just pop by tomorrow morning

SANDRO
Tomorrow—?

LORENZO
—morning, yes, say around eleven?

SANDRO
Wow, well / um—

LORENZO
I trust that's alright

SANDRO
I'm afraid I have brunch plans—

LORENZO
Cancel them
We'll toast the masterpiece

SANDRO
I'm just a little—shy about where it's / at, it's—

LORENZO
Sandro, come
You know I won't judge
But it better be fucking great

LORENZO points a finger at SANDRO and then chuckles.

SANDRO laughs, uncertain.

CLARICE reappears.

CLARICE
I can't find my car keys

LORENZO
Where're you going?
We haven't even had breakfast

CLARICE
I'm upset
I need to go for a drive

LORENZO
What the hell are you / so upset about?

CLARICE
Where are my keys?

LORENZO
Besides, you can't drive without a security detail, / you know that

CLARICE
Where are my fucking keys?

LORENZO
How the hell should I know?
Probably in that damn clamshell on the bookshelf

    CLARICE exits.

Mimosa?

SANDRO
No, I should be getting back
I have a lot of work to do

LORENZO
I love you like a brother, you know that?

SANDRO

You had your brother killed

LORENZO

I love you like the brother I never had and never killed

> *LORENZO smiles, squeezes SANDRO's shoulder.*

> *A spotlight appears on SANDRO.*

SANDRO

I ran all the way home
I could've had their driver take me
But no
I needed to run
I could've hailed a cab but I was already running
It was raining
I thought: good, I'm glad it's raining
Rain is appropriate
I ran through streets choked with protesters
and I thought: good, I'm glad they're screaming
Someone should be screaming

CHORUS
one-tenth
is a quarter
to the ears
one
seventh
of the face
at half
eyes
knee
breasts
from below
one third

The CHORUS repeats refrain during transition.

VII

SANDRO bursts into the studio.

LEONARDO is doing minor touch-ups on The Birth of Venus *canvas.*

SANDRO
She needs longer hair

LEONARDO
What?

SANDRO
Her hair's gotta cover her vagina

LEONARDO
I spent a week on that vagina

SANDRO
And you did a very commendable job, sweetie
for a man who's never seen one up close before
but the Medici's paying us a visit

LEONARDO
And?

SANDRO
I miscalculated

LEONARDO
You—

SANDRO
It was a test
That's it, isn't it, it was all a test to see if I would—

The commission
If Clarice and I would—

LEONARDO
What the hell are you saying?

SANDRO
And I failed, we failed

LEONARDO
But you knew he would see it

SANDRO
Yes I know I knew
But now

The details
It's too much

LEONARDO
But the nude was her idea

SANDRO
Yes yes she's testing him too and I'm right in the fucking—
Leo, I'm the only person in the world he thinks he can trust
and he just—
He needed to know if he really could

They consider the canvas.

LEONARDO
Maybe he won't mind

SANDRO
It's smut

LEONARDO
Yeah he'll probably mind

SANDRO
Absolutely fucking brilliant smut

LEONARDO
Does he want to see it before the summer?

SANDRO
No, sweetie, he's coming tomorrow morning

LEONARDO
What?

SANDRO
It's a nightmare, yes

LEONARDO
We could paint a dress over her

SANDRO
Don't be insane, that would completely destroy it

LEONARDO
Sandro

SANDRO
This is my masterpiece

LEONARDO
And you're prepared to go to jail for it?

SANDRO
If it comes to that

LEONARDO
You cry when you get paper cuts

SANDRO
This—this is my fucking soul

LEONARDO
Please

SANDRO
Every one of these paintings is a piece of my soul

LEONARDO
You're an atheist, you don't believe in souls

SANDRO
Exactly, so what else is there?
Beauty
It's the only sacred thing

LEONARDO
The only thing sacred to you is your cock
And your genius, maybe

SANDRO
My genius—
You cannot *be* genius
Beauty can only work through you
and holy shit she is working through me now, Leo
Venus alighting on the shore
the winds caressing her with a heavenly raiment of roses
It is the birth of love itself
It is working *through* me, Leo
like a direct line tapped right into the fucking cosmos
where no, there is no vengeful old god
where there is only sublime beauty and pleasure

And that is my duty
To defy ugliness and suffering
If I cannot live for at least that
then honestly? shoot me in the fucking face
This is bigger than me
And it's bigger than the Medici
We are not destroying this canvas
And we are not running away
At least I'm not and I hope to god you're with me

    Beat.

LEONARDO
I'm with you

SANDRO
Besides there's nothing about the painting that explicitly suggests I'm fuck-
    ing his wife

    Beat.

That said we should probably cover her vagina

LEONARDO
If we want to do it right it'll take days

SANDRO
We're doing it right

LEONARDO
But it's not just the hair I mean we have to move her entire left arm too
which then means repainting the entire raiment—

SANDRO
Leo

LEONARDO
There's just not enough time

SANDRO
Let me tell you what's going to happen
I'm going to open the cabernet sauvignon, alright
The *good* one
And you're going to mix me some ochre, cinnabar, red lake, and the purest
   virginal white
We're going to crack open the fresh brushes, put on some tunes,
and we're not stopping until fucking daybreak, got it?

   SANDRO turns to get started, but turns back when he realizes LEONARDO
   is still standing there.

Honey
It's time to werk!

   A nineties techno song begins to play as the men set to work.

   Flower petals fall from the sky as VENUS appears on a clamshell.

   She is singing the song, perhaps with the CHORUS as backup dancers
   in gold lamé booty shorts. It is an explosive, flamboyant stage image.

   Lights slowly fade on everything but VENUS's face.

   The song dies away. VENUS speaks.

VENUS
When I was a little girl everyone would say
Venus, you are the most sublime creature to ever walk the earth
And I said: cool, thanks
They said, Venus, your beauty outshines that of the sun
mortal men write poems and paint paintings in praise of your divine perfection
And I said: yeah I know

They said, Venus, we will make you the goddess of love and beauty
and your name will be hallowed for all of eternity
And I said: you know what, you really don't need to do that
The truth is I got bored of being beautiful, of beautiful things
of beautiful men singing beautiful songs to me
As I grew up I wanted nasty-ass fuckers
I wanted men with crooked teeth and bent cocks
into dirty talk and piss play in cheap motels
I wanted to make love to subhumans, to Neanderthal men
dragging their knuckles through dark back alleys
who could bite beer caps off bottles with their bare teeth
and tell you the year and make of a car by the sound of its engine
The worst, though, is being beautiful and young forever
Never getting fat, never getting wrinkled
never getting to feel the exquisite transcendence of death
Honestly?
I would trade beauty for death in a heartbeat

VIII

Lights rise once again on SANDRO's *studio. The dead of night. The two
men frantically work to finish the canvas.*

LEONARDO
What is it?

SANDRO
Do you smell something?

LEONARDO
No

SANDRO
It's almost like—

LEONARDO
Fuck it's already midnight

SANDRO
Open the window

LEONARDO
What?

SANDRO
Just open the window

LEONARDO gets up and opens the window.

LEONARDO
Whoa yeah I can sm—
Sandro

In the darkness we hear the voices of two boys singing, unseen.

BOY 1	BOY 2
And, lo, the smoke	And, lo, the smoke of the country
the smoke	
And, lo, the smoke of the country /	went up
as the smoke of a furnace	
And, lo, the smoke	And, lo, the smoke
And the Lord rained	And the Lord rained upon Sodom
And, lo, the smoke /	and upon Gomorrah
the smoke of the country went up /	brimstone and fire out of heaven
lo, the smoke /	and he overthrew those cities
And all the plain	And all the plain
And, lo, the smoke	And all the inhabitants of the cities
	and that which grew
upon the ground	upon the ground
And, lo, the smoke /	of the country went up
as the smoke of a furnace	

SANDRO goes over to the window. A spotlight appears. He speaks to the audience.

SANDRO
In the distance, smoke was rising from the piazza
It was the dead of night
but the flames lit the black plume from below
From where we stood we could not see the pyre
or the gathered mob
but we knew
It had started

LEONARDO
Are they—?

SANDRO
Yes

LEONARDO
That smell—

SANDRO
It's flesh

LEONARDO
The smell of burning—

SANDRO
Faggots

LEONARDO wretches.

LEONARDO
It's in my throat

SANDRO
Just stay calm

LEONARDO
You said the earth was round

SANDRO
Leo

LEONARDO
You said this was the fucking Renaissance

SANDRO
Leo, listen to me

LEONARDO
We're fucked

SANDRO
No

LEONARDO
You're the most flagrant sodomite in Florence
they're probably building your pyre as we speak

SANDRO
That is not constructive thinking

LEONARDO
We're so fucked

SANDRO
We are not / fucked, we just—

LEONARDO
We bet on the wrong horse

SANDRO
The Medici have an army
They have allies

LEONARDO
We need to get out of here

SANDRO
What's this "we"?
You can go whenever you want
I-I-I release you
What are you even worried about?

> *SANDRO points out the window.*

This?
Why should you get caught up in any of this?

LEONARDO
Just come with me

SANDRO
And go where?
Run back to your mother's farm?

LEONARDO
Why not?

SANDRO
And wallow with the pigs?
Eat potatoes until our teeth fall out?

LEONARDO
Better than getting them fucking / knocked out by a mob

SANDRO
If I run away I have nothing—

LEONARDO
Sandro

SANDRO
—I'm less than nothing

LEONARDO
This is fucking madness

SANDRO
That mob is not the whole city

LEONARDO
It doesn't matter

SANDRO
There are still more reasonable people in / this city than not and together—

LEONARDO
It doesn't matter! Where are they?!

SANDRO
—we are bigger than madness and we will not be afraid—

LEONARDO
But I am / I'm afraid

SANDRO
—and we will live however the fuck we want

LEONARDO
You think they won't throw your ass on the fire
because you can paint a few beautiful paintings?

SANDRO
The Medici are not going to let an angry mob / of-of-of fucking peasants—

LEONARDO
You don't get it, do you?
You're just another happy-go-lucky queer
A real *delight* to have around
Always a good quip, real life of the party
You're a prestige item for them, Sandro
Like a . . . a fancy armoire
And lucky you you've gained a bit of power
But don't forget you're a happy-go-lucky queer
We're as disposable as lapdogs

SANDRO
Where's my phone?

LEONARDO
What?

SANDRO
My phone

LEONARDO
How can you—?

SANDRO
Just help me find it!

> *LEONARDO realizes what SANDRO's thinking. He dashes over to the pile of sheets on the floor and finds the phone.*

LEONARDO
Here I—

> *LEONARDO glances down at the phone and cups his mouth.*

SANDRO
What?
What is it?

>   *A faint spot up on* POGGIO's *face.* SANDRO *crosses to* LEONARDO *and looks at the phone.*

POGGIO
Ten forty-nine
Missed call
Ten fifty
Missed call

Ten fifty
Missed call

Ten fifty-one
Turn on your phone girl
Bad news brewing

Ten fifty-three
Missed call

Ten fifty-seven
Shit's going down answer your fucking phone

>   *The* CHORUS *begin slamming faggots of wood into a giant pile at the centre of the stage.*

Eleven Missed call	**CHORUS** one seventh of a man
Eleven Missed call	is

Eleven
Missed call

Eleven o'two
Missed call

Eleven o'two
Missed call

Eleven o'four
For the love of god pick up pick up pick up

Eleven o'four
Missed call

Eleven o'four
Missed call

Eleven o'five
Love you

equal to the
head
and

knee

below the knee
is a quarter
is a half

The CHORUS *repeats this underneath.*

SANDRO & LEONARDO
(murmur) Love you

> SANDRO *breaks down in a fit of grief. He runs to the window sobbing.*
> LEONARDO *restrains him.* SANDRO *grows increasingly hysterical until*
> *there is a pounding at the door. They fall silent. The pounding comes*
> *again, this time louder. The two men hold each other, weeping.*

POGGIO
(off stage) Open up, you fuckers, I know you're in there

> SANDRO *is in disbelief.* LEONARDO *jumps up and runs to the door.*

POGGIO stumbles in. He is a ghost of himself.

SANDRO runs to POGGIO and hugs him as if he has come back from the dead.

After a long moment SANDRO pulls away.

SANDRO
Who are they?

POGGIO
I don't know yet
But at least I can strike you two fuckers off the list

POGGIO makes to leave.

SANDRO
Whoa whoa whoa where're you going?

POGGIO
Girl, you ain't my only friend

SANDRO
You can't go back out there

POGGIO
Verrocchio's not replying to my texts

SANDRO covers his mouth and nods, trying to contain himself. He hugs POGGIO one last time.

SANDRO
Be careful

POGGIO
No
The time for being careful's over

POGGIO exits.

SANDRO and LEONARDO are left together in a moment of silence, staring at one another.

LEONARDO
I wish you would just fucking hold me for a second

SANDRO comes up behind LEONARDO and embraces him, tentative at first, but then with greater insistence. Something in them releases. LEONARDO turns around and kisses SANDRO. The two men make out with a passionate, almost agonized frenzy, as if this might be the last pleasure they ever feel. As the lights fade, they strip one another bare.

Spotlight up on the face of MARIA.

Spoken softly and swiftly, underscoring:

MARIA
the length of the outspread arms is equal to the height of a man
from the hairline to the bottom of the chin is one-tenth of the height of a man
from below the chin to the top of the head is one-eighth of the height of a man
from above the chest to the top of the head is one-sixth of the height of a man
from above the chest to the hairline is one-seventh of the height of a man
the maximum width of the shoulders is a quarter of the height of a man
from the breasts to the top of the head is a quarter of the height of a man
the distance from the elbow to the tip of the hand is a quarter of the height of a man
the distance from the elbow to the armpit is one-eighth of the height of a man
the length of the hand is one-tenth of the height of a man
the root of the penis is at half the height of a man
the foot is one-seventh of the height of a man
from below the foot to below the knee is a quarter of the height of a man

from below the knee to the root of the penis is a quarter of the height of a man
the distances from below the chin to the nose and the eyebrows and the hairline are equal to the ears and to one-third of the face

As MARIA *speaks the lights slowly fade to black.*

End of Act I.

ACT II

I

Darkness.

CHORUS
one-tenth
to the root
of a man
is a quarter
to the top
of the height
top
one-third

eyes
knee
breasts

from above
is a quarter
chin to the nose
chin
chin to the nose
chin

one seventh
top of the head
of the face
from below
one third

is a half
top of the head
top
one

to the root
chin

equal to the ears
equal to the
nose

to the root
one-third
at half

one
tenth
of a man

from above
is a quarter
chin to the nose
chin
chin to the nose
chin

is a half
top of the head

top
one

> *During this choral sequence the lights raise faintly on* SANDRO'*s studio.* LEONARDO *is asleep, still naked, while* SANDRO *frantically works on the canvas in his underwear.*

> *A loud knocking.* SANDRO *bolts upright.*

SANDRO
You gotta be fucking joking

> LEONARDO *goes to the window and looks out.*

LEONARDO
Here we go

SANDRO
Already?

LEONARDO
Black limo

SANDRO
Fuck

> SANDRO *throws a cloth over the painting. They both flash about for a minute, frantically dressing.* LEONARDO *turns the canvas and easel around to face the audience.*

> *More knocking.*

LEONARDO
Just get the door

SANDRO
Alright, alright just pick up this shit

LEONARDO
Pants!

SANDRO
You get the door!

More knocking.

LEONARDO
—for fuck's sake—

LEONARDO exits to open the door.

SANDRO pulls his pants on.

CLARICE and LORENZO enter, LEONARDO trailing them.

LORENZO
Sandro!
I'm so excited I haven't slept a wink

SANDRO
Me neither

*SANDRO crosses to embrace LORENZO. He makes to embrace CLARICE but
ends up awkwardly shaking her hand. LORENZO bursts out laughing.*

LORENZO chuckles.

LORENZO
Look at you two
Like you're meeting for the first time

SANDRO
Would you like some coffee?

LORENZO
I don't drink coffee

SANDRO
Of course
I knew that
Like I said, I haven't slept

LORENZO
No sleep, no sleep for anyone
Did you know them?
The three men they burned?

SANDRO
Three

LORENZO
I wondered if they might be pals of yours from art school

SANDRO
What were their names?

LORENZO
I don't know, but we drove past on the way here
Those fuckers smashed the back window
Did I already mention that?

SANDRO
No

LORENZO
We're still a little shaken up

CLARICE
Can we make this quick?
I have a headache

LORENZO
Can you give me fifteen minutes?
In my whole goddamn day?
This is my life these days, Sandro
Five minutes for breakfast
Fifteen minutes for a friend
And then putting out fires till bedtime
Where's the fun? There's no time
So I assume it's that one over there?

LORENZO crosses to the canvas.

May I?

SANDRO
Before you do I just—

LORENZO pulls off the cloth that covers it.

The canvas is revealed in its full glory for the first time in the play. It is luminous.

Silence.

CLARICE
Well?
What do you think?

Pause.

Do you like it?

Pause.

LORENZO
Wow

CLARICE
I told you it's a little bit daring

LORENZO
I uh . . .
Wow

CLARICE
(to SANDRO) I see you've taken a little creative liberty with the hair

LORENZO
I can see why it has taken a lot of sittings
It's . . . a masterpiece

SANDRO
A—?
You mean you—?

 SANDRO laughs.

Jesus, I can't tell you how nervous I was for you to see it
I-I literally didn't sleep / a wink last night

LORENZO
I mean I can practically smell her she's so alive

SANDRO
Really

LORENZO
Do you know the smell I mean?
The earthy one
Like moss after a warm rain
With traces of talcum powder
Just looking at this painting I can smell it

CLARICE
I told you
It's a masterpiece

LORENZO
(to SANDRO) Do you know the smell I mean?

SANDRO
Can't say I do

LORENZO
It's the funniest thing
Seeing you like this

CLARICE
Naked?

LORENZO
So . . . content

CLARICE
I'm always content

LORENZO
Those eyes
I haven't seen those eyes in years

CLARICE
Don't be ridiculous
You see me every day

SANDRO
It's funny, I was worried she looked bored in the painting

SANDRO forces a laugh.

I mean after sitting for so long

LORENZO
(to CLARICE) Can I ask you a favour?

CLARICE
Of course you / can ask—

LORENZO
Lie down on your back

CLARICE chuckles.

CLARICE
What?

LORENZO
You heard me

CLARICE
. . .

LORENZO
I'm not going to ask you again

CLARICE
Why do you want / me to lie down on—

LORENZO
Funny, that's exactly what I remember
Even though it's been years

CLARICE
Lorenzo

LORENZO
The way you rest your hand like that over your breast
with your fingers gently splayed above the other breast
That's how you used to rest your hand when you were laying on your back, see
That's always how you rested your hand
always your right hand, just like that
after we fucked
Looking into each other's eyes
Isn't that funny?
That I should see that hand here again
The first time in . . . oh, what . . . four years
Did she tell you this is how we lay together, Sandro?
After we fucked
Her fingertips resting just above her left breast
How sweet of her to remember
how incredibly sexy and sentimental of her to relay this little gesture
Perhaps to rekindle the old fires, was that it, sweetie?
Or perhaps, Sandro, you happened to find yourself sketching my wife
    naked and on her back
Somehow, and I can't imagine how
splayed like this in perfect simulation of post-coital bliss

SANDRO
If I may—

> LORENZO *punches* SANDRO *in the face, knocking him to the ground.*
> CLARICE *screams and sits bolt upright.* SANDRO'S *nose gushes blood.*

> LORENZO *points at* LEONARDO.

LORENZO
You—
Fetch some ice

> *LEONARDO and SANDRO glance at one another, and in that brief instant something passes between them. CLARICE notices this. LEONARDO runs out of the studio.*

> *LORENZO pulls out his hunting knife.*

You know what I'd love, as your patron?
A peek at the great artist in action
Why don't you two pretend like I'm not here

> *Beat.*

Well—what are you waiting for?

CLARICE
Lorenzo—

LORENZO
Go on: fuck each other
Just pretend I'm not here

> *SANDRO and CLARICE do nothing.*

I said—

> *LORENZO lunges at SANDRO. They scuffle. CLARICE intercedes.*

Did you think this was a game of squash?
Did you think my wife was a little ball you could slam around the court?
A game you could beat me at and we'd pat each other on the back
and go for a cold beer afterwards?

CLARICE
Fuck you
Do not scrutinize me and do not—
You think this is about you, this is not about you
I am finally living and you can't stand it, can you?

LORENZO turns to SANDRO.

LORENZO
And what about you?
You love her?

SANDRO
No

LORENZO
(to SANDRO) Our hunting trips, everything I confided
When you twisted your ankle in Umbria
I carried you two hours *two hours* on my back
What was that?
I fucking loved I fucking trusted you I wanted to but I didn't and that's—
That's—

LORENZO points at his chest.

Do you know what I have in mind for you?
There is a windowless cell in the basement of my palace
with three feet of fetid water with pieces of shit bobbing in it
because this is where the latrines of the palace empty into, you see
like a sewer

LORENZO glances at CLARICE.

and I'm thinking:
how delightful it will be to hear your moans and screams every time I take a shit
to open the toilet seat and shout down at you in the pitch dark

and even long after you're dead and your corpse is devoured by the rats
and just your white bones are left bobbing in the water
I'll shout down, "Good day, friend, how's the weather down there?!"

CLARICE
Lorenzo—

LORENZO
Shut up

SANDRO
If I / might—

LORENZO
Did I say you could speak?
Put your mouth around my shoe
Go on, bite my shoe

> SANDRO *slowly gets to his knees and puts his mouth around* LOREN-
> ZO's *shoe.*

Snakes can't help their nature, can they?
They eat whatever hot-blooded thing they can get their mouths around
And yet sticking you down my toilet feels somehow . . . anticlimactic, doesn't it?
For a man of so many climaxes like yourself
It almost seems more fitting—an almost Biblical judgment
To cut off the evil at the root of the problem
Get up

> LORENZO *gives his foot a kick, causing* SANDRO *to exclaim in pain.*
> SANDRO *stands, his mouth bleeding.*

Pull down your pants

CLARICE
Lorenzo, stop it

LORENZO
I said pull down your pants!

SANDRO pulls down his pants.

Do you have . . . an erection?

SANDRO
I'm sorry, I—

LORENZO
Even now, you have a fucking erection?

SANDRO
One final salute, I suppose

LORENZO
I am doing you a favour, I hope you realize

SANDRO
I'm sure I'll see it that way one day

LORENZO
Take it out

CLARICE
Stop

LORENZO
Clarice, for / fuck's sake—

CLARICE
I swear to god I'll smash every window
in every car and house you own

LORENZO
He . . . you . . . have *hurt* me

CLARICE
So you want to hurt him?

LORENZO
I want—

CLARICE
To punish him?

LORENZO
Yes

CLARICE
Then take away the thing he loves

LORENZO
What do you think I'm doing?

CLARICE
Take the boy

SANDRO
What?

CLARICE
He loves the boy
So take something from him
Better yet
Buy some favour with the masses
Turn the boy over to the friar as the sodomite he is
Look! they'll say
The Medici clean house!

LORENZO
(to SANDRO) You see how my wife bargains with me?
She does this with everything
I want a black leather couch, she wants the white one
She'll say—
(to CLARICE) do you remember?
"If we get the white couch
you can have the granite countertop in the ensuite"
What do you say to that?

> *SANDRO doesn't answer.*

Is the boy your peace offering?

> *SANDRO doesn't answer. LORENZO presses the knife up to SANDRO's groin.*

	SANDRO
Speak up	*(whispers/gasps)* Yes

LORENZO
Pardon?

SANDRO
Yes

LORENZO
(to CLARICE) You get your white couch

> *LORENZO takes out a cellphone and dials a number.*

Yes, waylay the boy on his return
Leonardo
Yes
Put him in the toilet

LORENZO puts away his phone.

Well I must be going
Sorry for the short visit
Oh and—

Referring to the canvas:

no rush on finishing that up
I'm not sure we have room for it anyway

LORENZO makes to leave.

SANDRO
Can I see him?

LORENZO
Well of course you can
They burn them in public

LORENZO exits.

SANDRO and CLARICE are alone in the studio for a moment.

CLARICE exits.

For a long moment SANDRO does nothing. Then he throws a fit. He smashes a chair; he tears off his clothes. He trashes his studio.

The CHORUS begin singing the madrigal from the top of the show.

Naked, SANDRO begins throwing paint at The Birth of Venus *until it resembles a Jackson Pollock abstract.*

He then collapses on the ground, sobbing.

11

Darkness.

A faint spotlight appears on LEONARDO'*s face. He is naked, shivering, and his hands are handcuffed together. He is seated on the ground, as if in a prison cell.*

LEONARDO
Dear God, if I'm a sodomite, what are you?
If you made me in your image
and I'm an abomination, what are you?
If I'm a sodomite, what are you, God?
And where is my town
if you destroyed Sodom in a rain of fire
A stealth bomber over the desert
breaking the sound barrier
What are you if not a gravedigger?
If not a psychopath in the desert
If I am a sodomite, what the fuck are you?
What are you?
If I am, then what are you
If I am God
then what is
If I am
What is
If I am
I am
If I am
I am
I am
I am

III

Lights rise on SANDRO'S *studio. He is drunk and passed out, surrounded by half-empty wine bottles.*

MARIA *enters. She takes in the ravaged studio and rushes over to* SANDRO. *She tries to rouse him, but to no avail. She walks over to the workbench, grabs a small basin and a cloth, exits off stage, and returns with the basin filled with water.*

She proceeds to dump the basin of water over SANDRO'S *head. He bolts upright, gasping.*

MARIA *begins stripping off* SANDRO'S *shirt.*

MARIA
You're a mess

SANDRO
Jesus Christ what the / hell are you doing?

MARIA
Have you pissed yourself?

SANDRO
Just—

MARIA *removes* SANDRO'S *shirt and begins trying for his pants.*

MARIA
Baby, you should have called me

SANDRO
They took Leonardo

MARIA stops.

And I let them
They came and I just—

>   *SANDRO gestures as if to say "I just gave him away."*

>   *MARIA continues undressing SANDRO, pulling off his pants.*

Ma, would you just—

MARIA
They reek
Take them off

SANDRO
Do you think I care about—?

>   *She snaps her fingers.*

MARIA
Off

>   *SANDRO removes his pants. And begins to cry.*

>   *MARIA leaves with the clothes and the wash basin. She returns with
>   the basin, once again filled with cold water, but this time sudsy. She
>   holds a sponge.*

You let company use that washroom?
With pubes all over the toilet seat like that?

SANDRO
Ma

MARIA begins bathing SANDRO. She soaks the sponge in the soapy water and scrubs him down.

Ah ah ah ah that's cold

MARIA
It'll wake you up

MARIA bathes SANDRO for a few moments.

I knew something was wrong
I was dead asleep and I sat up and I knew I just
I sensed it

SANDRO
If you keep saying witchy shit like that they'll burn you too

MARIA
I'd like to see them try

They laugh.

Beat.

He's something special, isn't he?

SANDRO nods.

So what are you going to do?

SANDRO
It's too late

MARIA
If you think like that

SANDRO
I lost him

MARIA
When you were a teenager you started bringing boys and girls home to bed
Sometimes three or four at a time, remember?
And oh the noise you would all make!
And look, I gave a few winning blow jobs in my time
but you were out of control!
The neighbours would glare at me from behind their curtains
I cried to my priest: "Father, what should I do?"
He said: "You must show him the path; you must change his heart"
But I said: "Oh, you don't know my Sandro, there's no changing him"
He came out of the womb sucking his own cock
Well I didn't tell the priest that, but it's true

SANDRO
I know

MARIA
The priest told me I had a choice to make
"You can either continue to love this hopeless blasphemer
or you can pour your love into God"
And that's when I realized I loved God
But I loved my baby more
I loved God—but I loved you more
I chose you
And I never went back
And now you have to choose
between love and your god

SANDRO
C'mon, you know I don't believe in god

MARIA
The thing you worship

SANDRO
What are you / talking about?

MARIA
You know exactly what I'm talking about

Beat.

The time has come, Sandro
You have to make a choice

Lights shift.

I V

*Lights faintly rise again on SANDRO's studio. It is still trashed and lit-
tered with empty wine bottles.*

*SANDRO, dressed in a different shirt from earlier, busies himself trying
to restore some semblance of order to the chaotic space. He scoops up an
armful of wine bottles and exits into the next room to throw them out.*

POGGIO
(from off stage) Hello?
Anybody?

POGGIO enters the studio dressed as a nun. He surveys the damaged studio.

Oh my god

SANDRO re-enters and screams when he sees POGGIO.

It's just me, girl
Oh, babe

POGGIO holds him.

SANDRO
They—

POGGIO
I know
I heard

SANDRO pulls away.

SANDRO
What the hell's with the nun drag?

POGGIO
Honey, those bastards can spot a sodomite a mile away
Whattaya think they'll do if they see my flaming ass running through the streets?

SANDRO lifts up the hem of POGGIO's habit.

SANDRO
How'd you even get this?

POGGIO
Oh I've had it for years
I've worn it to parties, you've seen me
I stole it when Verrocchio and I were painting that fresco in Pistoia

SANDRO
Verrocchio, is he—?

POGGIO
They roughed him up pretty bad

SANDRO
No

POGGIO
He's okay for now but they'll come back for him
They're coming for all of us

POGGIO takes out a black robe for SANDRO.

Look, that's why I got you one of these sinister-ass robes

SANDRO
You can't / be serious

POGGIO
And there's no way you're leaving here without it
Everyone in the city knows your face

SANDRO
I can't leave

POGGIO
Sandro

SANDRO
I'm getting him back

POGGIO
I know, I know, babe, and we will, but I'm here to tell you—
while you've been fucking around with the Medici
Antonio and I've been hatching a plan to save our sorry asses, alright?

SANDRO
That's great, really, but it's too / late for me, I've already—

POGGIO
Anyone we think's a target we're getting them to five different safe houses
    across the city
A rich old client of mine from Arezzo's sending cars to each of the houses

They're picking us up tonight at ten o'clock sharp, alright
and we've / gotta be ready for them when they show

SANDRO
Babe, I wish I could, but I can't

POGGIO
I know you want to save Leo but if we try to bust him out now we could
blow the whole plan / and then everyone's fucked

SANDRO
I don't have time to go / to Arezzo with you and every queen in the city

POGGIO
Once we're at the safe house we can / coordinate from there

SANDRO
You need to go

POGGIO
I know, and those fuckers could be back at any minute
so just put on this fucking death frock and let's get outta here

    POGGIO begins trying to dress SANDRO in the black robe.

SANDRO
No, no you have to go *now*

POGGIO
I know, fuck, and I'm trying to / take you with me—

SANDRO
Right now, just go please, you / need to get out of here

POGGIO
—and every goddamn second we waste licking our wounds—

SANDRO
You don't understand, I—

SAVONAROLA appears in the doorway.

POGGIO
—risks fucking up everything, the entire plan, and there's a lot more—

POGGIO turns around, sees SAVONAROLA, and screams.

Fuckfuckfuck it's too late!

SANDRO
Just . . . listen to me—

POGGIO
(screaming at SAVONAROLA) Get out of here get the fuck out of here you think we're afraid of you / you piece of shit get *out*

SANDRO
Poggio

POGGIO
(to SAVONAROLA) Don't move don't you take a single fucking step closer you hear

SANDRO
Listen

SAVONAROLA
Botticelli, I suggest you get your barking guard dog under control

SANDRO
(to POGGIO) I invited him

POGGIO
What?

Beat.

SANDRO
I need to get Leo back

POGGIO
Uh huh

   Beat.

SANDRO
You have to understand—

POGGIO
Oh I understand things perfectly, thank you very much

   Beat.

This is some majorly fucked-up Faustian shit

SANDRO
Babe

POGGIO
Don't "babe" me
You're selling us out

SANDRO
I'm just trying to—

POGGIO
Don't you get it?
When you sell out to him you sell us all out

SANDRO
I'm sorry

POGGIO
I will hide
But I will not grovel
Goodbye, Sandro

> *POGGIO exits, making a wide arch around* SAVONAROLA *as he goes.*

> SANDRO *tries to call after* POGGIO *but there is nothing left to say.*

> *Silence.*

SANDRO
Can I get you something to drink?

SAVONAROLA
No

SANDRO
Chamomile tea perhaps?

> SAVONAROLA *takes in the studio.*

SAVONAROLA
So this is where it all happens
Your *genius*

> SAVONAROLA *points to* The Birth of Venus *canvas.*

What on earth happened to this one?

SANDRO
It's a new style I'm toying with

SAVONAROLA
Huh

SANDRO

I didn't know if my message would reach you

SAVONAROLA

Yes

Well

I have to admit I was pleasantly surprised to receive your invitation

I was wondering when I would have the pleasure

SANDRO

I can't imagine you've had much in your life

SAVONAROLA smirks in spite of himself.

SAVONAROLA

Is it true what they say?

That you've had a thousand lovers

SANDRO

Mmm . . . I think you might have an old source

SAVONAROLA

And does this give your life meaning?

This wanton pursuit of flesh?

Seems rather bereft

SANDRO

And how about burning people?

That really gets you out of bed in the morning, huh?

SAVONAROLA

I'm as upset by the burnings as you are

SANDRO

Oh really?

Well lucky for you, last time I checked they were burning faggots, not friars

SAVONAROLA

And how long before the wind changes direction
and we're all consumed by the fires?
You have me all wrong if you think I want to see anyone burned

SANDRO

But you are fanning the flames

SAVONAROLA

This is the people's revolution

SANDRO

Which you started

SAVONAROLA

The Medici brought this upon themselves
And I'm sorry if you happen to be collateral / in this but—

SANDRO

They are burning faggots in Piazza della Signoria because of your sermons

SAVONAROLA

I never told anyone / to burn anyone

SANDRO

The city is sick with the / pestilence of sin

SAVONAROLA

Yes, but I never—

SANDRO

And like Sodom and Gomorrah, its day of reckoning is near!

SAVONAROLA

Do you berate all your guests like this?
You invited me over, I am a very busy man.

SANDRO
I know, I—

SAVONAROLA
Do I want you to burn on the pyre? Of course not
Do I want to save the souls of this city? Yes
And I believe they can be, every last one of them
None of us are beyond redemption
Not even you

SANDRO
Spare Leonardo

SAVONAROLA
Remind me, which / one is he—?

SANDRO
The boy being held in the Medici's toilet

SAVONAROLA
Right

SANDRO
Collect Leonardo from the Medici and let him go
I'm begging you

SAVONAROLA
The people want a burning

SANDRO
If you could just reason with them

SAVONAROLA
You can't reason with a mob

SANDRO
You have influence
They listen to you

SAVONAROLA
Botticelli—

SANDRO
Tell me what you want
I can make it worth your while

SAVONAROLA
Are you bargaining with me?

SANDRO
I know how the world works

SAVONAROLA
But do you understand how God works?

SANDRO
If there is a god he will spare Leonardo

   Beat.

Tell me what you want

   Pause.

SAVONAROLA
I want you to publicly denounce the Medici

SANDRO
Done

SAVONAROLA
And burn your paintings

SANDRO
Burn—

SAVONAROLA
Your entire studio
Offer each and every one of your paintings to the bonfire

SANDRO
But—

SAVONAROLA
And then, Botticelli, you will renounce painting altogether
and pledge your allegiance to my cause

SANDRO
When you say "renounce"—?

SAVONAROLA
Throw every one of your brushes
every pot of paint and canvas you own into the fire
You will publicly pledge to never paint again for as long as you live
Renounce your ways

Renounce all vice
and declare you have seen the light
This is a trade I would consider
If the greatest sinner of all can be saved in front of the masses
then anything is possible

> SANDRO *paces the studio, taking in each one of his canvases as if they were his children.*

> *A long, anxious, ruminating silence.*

And in exchange I'll spare the boy

> *SANDRO is silent. Agonized.*

> *He wrestles with the fate of his soul.*

> *Time passes.*

I suggest you make up your mind quickly

> *Through tears SANDRO turns to SAVONAROLA and smiles.*

SANDRO
Burn them

SAVONAROLA
Burn them?

SANDRO
Burn all of them

SAVONAROLA
You want to / burn them?

SANDRO
I want to . . . to . . . throw them into the fucking fire

SAVONAROLA
I see

SANDRO
Just give me a stick and some marshmallows

SAVONAROLA
That's quite the about-face

SANDRO
I have—seen the light

SAVONAROLA points his finger at SANDRO, thinking.

SAVONAROLA
It's good
It's a good start
But uh—
Still
I'm not quite sure it's—

SANDRO
Enough?

SAVONAROLA
Well it doesn't really have the same impact, does it?
A few paintings
The people have come to expect a certain—
I'm just not sure it drives home the point in quite the same way

SANDRO
Then burn more

SAVONAROLA
More?

SANDRO
Everything
Every occasion of sin

SAVONAROLA
Oh?

SANDRO
Books
For instance

SAVONAROLA
Books?

SANDRO
Musical instruments and and and sheet music

SAVONAROLA
Yes

SANDRO
Porn, cosmetics, jewels, uh uh fancy dresses

SAVONAROLA
The Greek manuscripts

SANDRO
All the heretical writings

SAVONAROLA
Yes yes

SANDRO
Costumes and masks

SAVONAROLA
Tapestries

SANDRO
People could offer up their own possessions

SAVONAROLA
Self-elected

SANDRO
A-a-a great purging!

SAVONAROLA
Fed by the flames of your paintings

SANDRO
Just—use them as kindling

SAVONAROLA
A great bonfire

SANDRO
A bonfire of the vanities

SAVONAROLA
Yes
Yes yes yes
Or what if we called it—?
No that's good
A Bonfire of the Vanities
Tomorrow at sunrise you will throw your paintings onto the pyre

SANDRO
Every one

    SAVONAROLA points to the destroyed The Birth of Venus *canvas.*

SAVONAROLA
Except that one, that's a piece of shit

SANDRO
In exchange for Leonardo

SAVONAROLA
What?
Oh yes . . . I'll see what I can do

Blackout.

V

A deep rumbling. The rumbling begins to deepen, grows louder, becomes something verging on the tectonic, like the sound of the earth rupturing.

A bonfire blazes.

CHORUS 1	CHORUS 2
the arms	
	one-tenth
the chin	one-eighth
the head	
	one-sixth
the chest	one-seventh
the hairline	a quarter
the shoulders	
the eyebrows	
the breasts	
the elbow	
	one-eighth
the armpit	a quarter
the hand	
the penis	one-seventh
the foot	
the knee	
	a quarter

the chin
.the nose   one-third
the ears

   The CHORUS *repeat softly underneath.*

   SANDRO *appears, holding several of his canvases. His silhouette looms*
   large in the blaze of the fire.

   The sounds of a crowd, cheering.

   SANDRO *is silent for a moment, steeling himself. He picks up a micro-*
   phone attached to an amp, the same used by SAVONAROLA *in Act 1.*

SANDRO
I wanted to say
If I might . . .
There was once a great fire within me
But I have come to realize that my paintings are . . . nothing
but sinful, earthly distractions
I mean look at this one
Pure pagan propaganda

   He points to a painting:

Nothing but flesh
I never noticed how gauzy those gowns were
Do they need to be so . . . sheer and sensuous?
I mean her breasts are basically pouring out
And look: Mercury is barely wearing that sheet
He's on full display
Yeah, there's no denying it, it's just a garden of flesh

   He turns to another painting:

And my god where do I even start with this one?
Those cherubs . . . are clearly devils
The horns, the cloven hooves
Those little devil lips blowing into Mars's ear
makes him throw his head back in ecstasy—he's spent
The jugular exposed
We follow that line, which leads us down his perfectly taught chest
Past his jutting hip
All the way to his hand, clearly indicating the main focus of the painting
clearly positioned as if holding an imaginary cock
Like if you squint it's like he's holding his cock
It's all so obvious

He turns to another painting:

Even the religious ones—look
St. Sebastian, pierced by arrows—why does he look orgasmic?
And this one
The Virgin Mary
The Mother of God
And her nipples are erect?
Her nipples are erect!
Like who did I think I was fooling?
Forgive me
For giving life to these visions
By my hand they were born
And by my hand they will die

The roar of the flames and the crowd climax.

Blackout.

The choral madrigal from the top of the show resumes.

Faces appear, faintly illuminated in the dark.

MARIA
We walked home in silence

CLARICE
What became of Botticelli?

SAVONAROLA
He had a crisis of faith

MARIA
And he didn't cry

CLARICE
Stopped painting, as far as I know

POGGIO
I don't want to hear that name

CLARICE
He faded into obscurity

LORENZO
Florence was blue-balled for years after

SAVONAROLA
Consider for a moment, if you will—

MARIA
I tied his hands to the bars of the crib

SAVONAROLA
—what we were trying to achieve

CLARICE
I prefer not to think about it

LORENZO
I mean it's nothing really new, is it?
There's always a plague
There's always a fire

POGGIO
Ave, o Maria, piena di grazia

MARIA
I loved him like any mother

CLARICE
I said I prefer not to think about it

V I

Lights up faintly on SANDRO'*s studio. It is completely bare except for*
The Birth of Venus *canvas, propped up against the back wall. The*
Jackson Pollock–style paint splatters have mostly been wiped away,
revealing much of the completed canvas below. He sits alone for a
long moment in silence.

SANDRO
(to audience) You can't possibly hate me more than I hate myself
So save your judgment
I don't need your pity either
You might be watching this and thinking:
well obviously the Medici were going down
Obviously Florence would fall to the zealots
Nah uh, take it from me—
it's not as easy to tell when you're on the precipice as you might think
We convince ourselves things will more or less stay the course
That progress is a forward—

LEONARDO, gaunt and damp, enters.

SANDRO leaps to his feet but LEONARDO takes a step back. SANDRO does not want to be touched. A moment of silence.

LEONARDO
Don't—
I thought you were—

    Beat.

When they let me out I ran to the piazza
I saw what was left of the fire and I—
I really thought that you were—

    LEONARDO coughs up some blood.

SANDRO
You must be starving
Do you want me to make / you something to eat?

LEONARDO
I came for my backpack. Have you seen it around?

    SANDRO does a cursory scan of the empty room.

SANDRO
No

LEONARDO
Fuck
Had my passport in it

    Pause.

Are we all just playthings to you?
Huh?
Cum rags to keep you company?
Things to keep around to laugh at your jokes
fawn over your genius
and then fuck every once in a while
and then put back in the cupboard?
Or do you fuck because you can no longer feel love
just cheap sensation
Frankly, I think you've forgotten how to love anything but yourself
You find no human quite so alluring as your own genius
so we'll just have to be your disposable substitutes until you do

SANDRO
I'm sorry

LEONARDO
You're sorry

SANDRO
I burned everything for you

    LEONARDO begins a slow clap for him.

LEONARDO
Go suck a bag of dicks

    LEONARDO turns to go.

SANDRO
Wait
Where will you go?

LEONARDO
I'll find my way

SANDRO
Please just—

LEONARDO coughs up more blood.

LEONARDO
The palace is empty

SANDRO
And the Medici—?

LEONARDO
Fled, yes
Or perhaps they're just on vacation

Beat.

And look—I guess they left their fancy armoire behind

SANDRO
I'm fine

LEONARDO
I killed and ate a rat with my bare hands

SANDRO
I'm sorry

LEONARDO
You already fucking said that

Beat.

When I came to this city I sought you out
I fell madly in love with you
I wanted to be with you
I wanted to *be* you

SANDRO
Let me kiss you

LEONARDO
I have the plague

SANDRO
I don't care

    LEONARDO looks around the studio and notices The Birth of Venus
    canvas.

LEONARDO
How in god's name is that still here?

SANDRO
I disguised it

LEONARDO
How?

SANDRO
Threw a bunch of paint on it

LEONARDO
Are you going to finish it?

SANDRO
I renounced painting

LEONARDO

Oh don't give me that
The day the people have had enough
and they throw Savonarola on that fire
you're going to get right back at it
painting your nymphs and satyrs
So you lost a few years' work
A few beautiful pictures

SANDRO

A few beautiful pictures

    Silence.

LEONARDO

Do you even know how it ends for Venus?
The goddess of love?
Vulcan finds her and Mars in bed
and throws a scalding iron net overtop of them, trapping them for eternity
as all the gods of Olympus gather round and laugh at them

    Silence.

You've run out of words?
Jokes?
Your old shit isn't working anymore?

SANDRO

I . . . am a horrible person

    Silence.

I—

LEONARDO turns to leave. Lights shift. A spotlight appears on SANDRO as he turns to the audience.

For the historians in the audience
This is the moment where, without saying a word
Leonardo turned and walked out of my life forever

Beat.

But you know what, this is my damn play
and the historians, I'm sorry, y'all can go fuck yourselves

Tonight we finish this
The way it should have been
With all of you as my witnesses

Lights shift.

SANDRO and LEONARDO have repositioned themselves back into the scene.

Silence.

LEONARDO
You've run out of words?
Jokes?
Your old shit isn't working anymore?

SANDRO
I . . . am a horrible person

Silence.

I—
I love you
I love you
Do you hear me?
I love you
Profoundly
More than I thought humanly possible
Every shade and hue by your hand
I can't look at a colour without seeing your hand in it
Your eyes, your lips
I love you
And and maybe I can't express it but I'm trying
I want to spend every fucking day with you
Even if it is in some godforsaken stable in Vinci

> *LEONARDO stops. He looks back.*

You need to eat something

LEONARDO
I'm not hungry

> *SANDRO removes a floorboard and pulls out a jar of peanut butter, a knife, and a loaf of plain white bread.*

> *SANDRO makes a peanut butter sandwich and cuts it in two. LEONARDO walks over and sits down beside him. SANDRO hands one half of the sandwich to LEONARDO.*

> *They eat.*

SANDRO
Was it worth it?

LEONARDO
Was what worth it?

SANDRO
All these hellfires for a bit of buggery?

LEONARDO
I'm not afraid
I have seen the void
And I am not afraid

> *LEONARDO pulls the knife out of the jar of peanut butter and licks it slowly. SANDRO then puts his hand over LEONARDO's and licks the knife. They look at each other, holding the knife between them.*

> *Blackout.*

> *End of play.*

Sunday in Sodom

1 And there came two angels to Sodom at even; and Lot sat in the gate of Sodom: and Lot seeing them rose up to meet them; and he bowed himself with his face toward the ground;

2 And he said, Behold now, my lords, turn in, I pray you, into your servant's house, and tarry all night, and wash your feet, and ye shall rise up early, and go on your ways. And they said, Nay; but we will abide in the street all night.

3 And he pressed upon them greatly; and they turned in unto him, and entered into his house; and he made them a feast, and did bake unleavened bread, and they did eat.

4 But before they lay down, the men of the city, even the men of Sodom, compassed the house round, both old and young, all the people from every quarter:

5 And they called unto Lot, and said unto him, Where are the men which came in to thee this night? bring them out unto us, that we may know them.

6 And Lot went out at the door unto them, and shut the door after him,

7 And said, I pray you, brethren, do not so wickedly.

8 Behold now, I have two daughters which have not known man; let me, I pray you, bring them out unto you, and do ye to them as is good in your

eyes: only unto these men do nothing; for therefore came they under the shadow of my roof.

9 And they said, Stand back. And they said again, This one fellow came in to sojourn, and he will needs be a judge: now will we deal worse with thee, than with them. And they pressed sore upon the man, even Lot, and came near to break the door.

10 But the men put forth their hand, and pulled Lot into the house to them, and shut to the door.

11 And they smote the men that were at the door of the house with blindness, both small and great: so that they wearied themselves to find the door.

12 And the men said unto Lot, Hast thou here any besides? son in law, and thy sons, and thy daughters, and whatsoever thou hast in the city, bring them out of this place:

13 For we will destroy this place, because the cry of them is waxen great before the face of the Lord; and the Lord hath sent us to destroy it.

14 And Lot went out, and spake unto his sons in law, which married his daughters, and said, Up, get you out of this place; for the Lord will destroy this city. But he seemed as one that mocked unto his sons in law.

15 And when the morning arose, then the angels hastened Lot, saying, Arise, take thy wife, and thy two daughters, which are here; lest thou be consumed in the iniquity of the city.

16 And while he lingered, the men laid hold upon his hand, and upon the hand of his wife, and upon the hand of his two daughters; the Lord being merciful unto him: and they brought him forth, and set him without the city.

17 And it came to pass, when they had brought them forth abroad, that he said, Escape for thy life; look not behind thee, neither stay thou in all the plain; escape to the mountain, lest thou be consumed.

18 And Lot said unto them, Oh, not so, my Lord:

19 Behold now, thy servant hath found grace in thy sight, and thou hast magnified thy mercy, which thou hast shewed unto me in saving my life; and I cannot escape to the mountain, lest some evil take me, and I die:

20 Behold now, this city is near to flee unto, and it is a little one: Oh, let me escape thither, (is it not a little one?) and my soul shall live.

21 And he said unto him, See, I have accepted thee concerning this thing also, that I will not overthrow this city, for the which thou hast spoken.

22 Haste thee, escape thither; for I cannot do anything till thou be come thither. Therefore the name of the city was called Zoar.

23 The sun was risen upon the earth when Lot entered into Zoar.

24 Then the Lord rained upon Sodom and upon Gomorrah brimstone and fire from the Lord out of heaven;

25 And he overthrew those cities, and all the plain, and all the inhabitants of the cities, and that which grew upon the ground.

26 But his wife looked back from behind him, and she became a pillar of salt.

Sunday in Sodom premiered at Canadian Stage's Berkeley Street Theatre, Toronto, in rep with *Botticelli in the Fire* between April 26 and May 15, 2016, with the following cast and creative team:

Chris: Salvatore Antonio
Edith: Valerie Buhagiar
Sahrah: Nicola Correia-Damude
Isaac: Stephen Jackman-Torkoff
Derek: Christopher Morris
Lot: Alon Nashman

Director: Estelle Shook
Set and Costume Design: James Lavoie
Lighting Design: Steve Lucas
Composition and Sound Design: Samuel Sholdice
Projection Consultant: Cameron Davis
Fight Director: Simon Fon
Stage Manager: Michael Sinclair
Assistant Stage Manager: Andrea Baggs
Associate Technical Director: Bryan Steele
Props Bulder: Vanessa Janiszewski
Carpenter: Peter Velocci
Production Assistant: Melanie Hall
Head of Wardrobe: Ming Wong

Lights rise on EDITH.

She stands still, facing the audience. She does not move from her position for the entire play. Indeed, she has no movement whatsoever.

EDITH
I looked back
I did
I admit, I stopped running and I looked back

What an impertinent woman
Feeble-minded
Meek of heart
Or perhaps it's meek of spirit or some bullshit like that
Wasn't she told to run and not look back?
Why didn't she do what she was told?
I admit, I've never been much good at that

Yes I looked back
Because I was not one of God's chosen creatures
Because I had sin in my heart
I looked back because I suddenly remembered I had left the stove on
I looked back because I thought I heard the roar of laughter of everyone
   in the village
I looked back because of the eerie silence
Because a scorpion crossed my path and I was frightened

Because I couldn't bear to look at the back of my husband's righteous neck
   a second longer
Because I forgot to take my favourite porcelain bowl

Oh fuck off
I mean really
I looked back and turned to a pillar of salt
Our whole village was ground into salt
If that's what you prefer to call it
What do you call a body when it is no longer a body?
A building when it is no longer a building?
Bones and rubble, ground into salt

But really, what do they know?
The men who wrote the accounts
They weren't even there the day it happened
Do they even know it was a Sunday?
I bet not
I bet the day of the week never even crossed their minds
Or that there were people just going about their lives

That Sunday I did the wash, like I always do
In the village there is a basin where the women gather and gossip
We know all of each other's dirty laundry
I always have to be discreet because my husband Lot
is rather old and incontinent and leaves little surprises for me in his underwear
The other women always pretend not to notice but I know they do
Perhaps my husband does this in protest for some transgression or other
Like a cat might on a rug
Perhaps for forgetting to put milk in his tea that morning
Or putting my cold feet against his back in the night when he is snoring
   too loudly

I also wash my daughter Sahrah's bras and her baby girls' diapers
and also the diapers of dear old Nanna, Lot's mother, deaf and blind as a
   doorknob

I'm in what you'd call the Sandwich Generation
though it feels more like the Club Sandwich Generation
a great stack of mouths to feed and asses to wipe

My right hand is my ass-wiping hand
It also happens to be the hand I wear my wedding ring on
Once, while I was wiping Nanna's ass
I noticed that the small diamond in the ring had fallen out
Then, a week or so later, while we were eating dinner, she started to choke
I slapped her on the back and she coughed up the diamond
The village declared it a miracle from God and held a feast in her honour
Who was I to rain on the parade?

As I walked back from the washing basin my cellphone began to ring
I hate my cellphone
It was a gift from Lot but he's the only one who calls me
usually to ask me to pick him up something or other at the market
But all the same, I put my basket down
and rummage through my pockets for the damn phone

Lights appear faintly on ISAAC. *He is crying.*

Yes?

ISAAC
Aunt Edith?

EDITH
Who is this?

ISAAC
It's Isaac

EDITH
Isaac, sweetie, what's wrong?

ISAAC
My father tried to kill me

EDITH
What?
Are you alright?

ISAAC
Yeah I . . . think so

EDITH
What did Abraham do now?

ISAAC
He asked me to go for a walk with him up the mountain
and when we got to the top he pushed me onto this rock and he pushed
    me down

EDITH
He pushed you down?

ISAAC
Yeah
and then he took out a large knife
and held it to my throat like he was going to slit it

EDITH
Oh my God

ISAAC
And then he . . . it's like he snapped out of it or something
He just started crying and shaking his head
and hugging and kissing me

EDITH
He's lost it

ISAAC
He was apologizing
He said God had told him to do it

EDITH
And what, did his God just change his mind at the last minute?

ISAAC
I'm scared

EDITH
Of course, sweetie, where are you right now?

ISAAC
I'm in the washroom

EDITH
Are you at home?

ISAAC
Yeah

EDITH
Who's there with you?
Is your mother home?

ISAAC
Yeah she's in the kitchen

EDITH
Does she know what happened?

ISAAC
I don't know

EDITH
I think you should tell her
I'm sure she would be / very upset about this

ISAAC
I can't

EDITH
Why not, sweetie?

ISAAC
He's here too

EDITH
I see

ISAAC
He'd lose it

EDITH
Are any of your brothers home?

ISAAC
I don't know
I'm scared

EDITH
I know, sweetie

ISAAC
I don't know if I can stay here, I . . .
I'm worried he might . . .

>   *Beat.*

EDITH
Isaac?

ISAAC
Yeah

EDITH
You're worried he might hurt you?

ISAAC
Yeah

EDITH
Listen to me, sweetie, you can come stay with us for a few days
Would you like that?

ISAAC
Yeah

EDITH
I can make up the pullout bed for you
Isaac?
Are you there?

ISAAC
(whispers) I have to go

EDITH
Isaac, I'll meet you at the bus station at noon today, okay?
Isaac?

Lights fade on ISAAC.

Lot's uncle Abraham is a cult leader
A few years back he began saying that God spoke to him
and that he was to be the father of God's chosen people

I think quite obviously he's paranoid schizophrenic
but Lot's family is very traditional; they're not particularly well-educated
and there's lots of stigma around mental illness
Whenever I try to bring it up with my husband, we get into a big fight

Lights rise faintly on LOT.

He's not well

LOT
Would you just leave him alone?

EDITH
I just think he should see a specialist in / the city and at least get an assessment

LOT
Don't forget he bought us this house

EDITH
I'm not saying he's not generous
I'm just / concerned for his deteriorating mental health

LOT
And Sarah really likes you, she's a big fan of yours
I don't know why you have to pry into their personal business

EDITH
That Sunday I arrived home and hung the wet laundry on the line
My stomach was in knots
All I could think about was poor Isaac on that rock
Lot was in the kitchen watching news about the war
With his bad hip all he does these days
is watch the news and get himself worked up about it

(to LOT) I got a call from Isaac on my way back from the wash

LOT
What's that?

EDITH
Turn that down
I'm not going to shout at you across the kitchen

    LOT turns down the volume.

I said I got a call from Isaac

LOT
Who?

EDITH
Abraham's son

LOT
Which one?

EDITH
With the curly black hair

LOT
You'll have to be more / specific than that

EDITH
The one you call "Mincing Mary"

    He chuckles.

LOT
Oh yes yes

EDITH
Apparently Abraham dragged him to a mountaintop
and put a dagger to his throat
He started crying and begging for forgiveness

LOT
Who started crying, Abraham or / the boy?

EDITH
Abraham
Mind you I'm sure they both were
Anyway, he didn't slit the boy's throat, thank God
But naturally Isaac's traumatized
and I told him he could sleep on our couch until this blows over

LOT
What?

EDITH
Just for a few days
It's very tense / in their house right now

LOT
You just offered without asking me?

EDITH
He called me sobbing, what / could I say?

LOT
Goddammit, Edith—no, no way
The boy is not sleeping on our couch

EDITH
He's on a bus!

LOT
Too fucking bad!

EDITH
He has nowhere else to go!

LOT
Did you ever stop to think what kind of position this puts me in?
With Abraham?

EDITH
He doesn't have to know

LOT
Of course he'll—
Christ, don't be so stupid; he'll call around looking for his son
and what do you think he'll do when he finds out we're harbouring him

EDITH
Harbouring—

LOT
On our couch

EDITH
—he's not a terrorist, for / Christ's sake
using this CNN language

LOT
I can't believe—you can be so impulsive sometimes
You've got us in a real mess

EDITH
Oh have I?

LOT
Yes, you have

EDITH
And no one's blaming Abraham for the knife business

LOT
We don't know his side of the story

EDITH
He's coming to stay on our couch and that's that

LOT
Is it?

EDITH
Yes

LOT
And while you and Sahrah are menstruating
It's haram to have male visitors

EDITH
He's family!

LOT
It's haram

EDITH
The red curtain is up
You and Isaac stay on your side and we'll stay on ours

LOT
The neighbours will talk

EDITH
Please

LOT
Having a male visitor while you and Sahrah are on the rag?

EDITH
Oh don't use that expression, you know I hate it

LOT
What, on / the rag?

EDITH
You didn't seem to care about the neighbours
when you installed that massive godawful satellite dish

LOT
Oh don't bring the satellite dish into this

EDITH
This conversation is finished
Isaac is coming
You can turn up the volume on your war

Lights fade on LOT.

Sahrah was home doing double duty: breastfeeding and studying
Plus her menstrual cramps were hitting hard
I made her a ginger-root tea and carried it into her room

Lights up on SAHRAH.

SAHRAH
What's dad getting himself worked up about now?

EDITH
Isaac's coming to stay for a couple of days

SAHRAH
Did he finally drop the bombshell?

EDITH
What bomb?

SAHRAH
Bombshell
To his dad, about being a homo

EDITH
Homo*sexual*?

SAHRAH
No, *Homo sapiens*
Yes of course homosexual

EDITH
Our little Isaac?

SAHRAH
I keep forgetting you guys don't have Facebook

EDITH
How are the cramps?

SAHRAH
They're doing great
I'm in agony

EDITH
No wonder you're uncomfortable
you have that giant textbook pressing against you

SAHRAH
I have four exams pressing against me
that's why I'm / uncomfortable

EDITH
Four?
Next week?

SAHRAH
One two three four, yup

EDITH
Do you want me to help?

SAHRAH
Help?

EDITH
I don't know, ask you questions?

SAHRAH
About masters-level chemical engineering?

EDITH
Well

SAHRAH
That's sweet / but—

The sound of a baby crying.

Shit, I just put her down
Did your breasts ever hurt this much?
My breasts are killing me

EDITH
She probably needs a diaper change
I can do it

SAHRAH
It's okay, Mom, I got it

EDITH
No, no, you're studying

SAHRAH
Mom, / I

EDITH
It's fine, / I

SAHRAH
I said I *got it*

EDITH
There's no need to / take that tone with me

SAHRAH
I'm sorry, I just—

EDITH
I'm just trying to / help—

SAHRAH
I know, Mom, and you're—
You don't have to take on everyone's problems
I can take care of diapers

EDITH
Okay

SAHRAH
Sorry

EDITH
What?

SAHRAH
I feel like I'm always snappy with you these days

Beat.

You know what I was thinking, just this morning?
Do you remember how I used to scream at you that you ruined my whole
  complete life?

EDITH
Uh huh

SAHRAH imitates her younger self:

SAHRAH
You ruined my whole complete life

She laughs.

Oh my God what a little bitch

Beat.

Anyway, I was just thinking about that

EDITH
That I ruined your whole / complete life?

SAHRAH laughs.

SAHRAH
No, that obviously I knew you were doing your best but
I just never, like I don't have a memory of ever telling you that

EDITH
That

SAHRAH
that I knew you were . . . doing your best
and that you didn't ruin my whole complete life

EDITH
I can't stand this crying baby any longer

SAHRAH
Leave it, I've got it

    Lights fade on SAHRAH.

EDITH
I whiled away the morning doing various chores, I can't remember what
I went into the living room and unfolded the pullout couch
I put a fresh pair of sheets on the mattress, laid a quilt overtop
and slipped a new pillowcase over the pillow

    Lights rise on LOT.

LOT
It's too soon

EDITH
What?

LOT
To make the couch a bed

EDITH

You never sit on this couch

LOT

Well if I wanted to, now I can't
It's already a bed and it's not even the afternoon
What if we have company?

EDITH

They can sit at the kitchen table!

LOT

It's too soon for the bed

EDITH

Well it's a bed now
I'm going out to pick up Isaac

>   *Lights fade on* LOT.

I put on my sandals and, before leaving the house
I checked the mirror to make sure I didn't have any sleep in my eyes
or boogers dangling from my nose or some such thing
As I walked through the streets I suddenly became aware of something
    being . . . off
I looked around and realized the streets were deserted
Why was everything so quiet?
Well I suppose it *was* Sunday
And it was hot; in fact it was blisteringly hot, so perhaps that was it
I arrived at the bus station a couple of minutes before noon
and Isaac was already there, waiting for me

>   *Lights up on* ISAAC.

It came early
That's unusual

ISAAC
They bypassed Gomorrah

EDITH
But it's the bigger of the two towns

ISAAC
Didn't you hear about the bomb?

EDITH
What?

ISAAC
A car bomb went off in the market about an hour ago

EDITH
Oh my God, were there casualties?

ISAAC
They're not sure
I mean yes
But not sure how many

EDITH
Well I'm glad you got here in one piece
Do your parents know where you are?

ISAAC
No, I just left

EDITH
You're just having one terrible day, aren't you?

ISAAC
And it's not even noon

EDITH
Well it's only got room to get better
Isaac and I ran through the streets until we arrived back at the house

Lights faintly rise on LOT.

What the hell's the point of you watching the news 24-7
if you're not going to tell me a car bomb went off two miles away?

LOT
What, do you think there's going to be five or six car bombs going off
from here to the bus station?

EDITH
The streets are empty!
People are being cautious!

LOT
People are like mice, / one scurries they all scurry

EDITH
You want me killed!

LOT
Oh please

EDITH
Just because I made the couch / into a bed

LOT
You're being hysterical

Lights faintly rise on SAHRAH.

SAHRAH
What's going on?

LOT
Terrorists detonated a car bomb in the market

SAHRAH
Holy shit

ISAAC
In Gomorrah

SAHRAH
Hi, Isaac

EDITH
We don't know / they were terrorists

ISAAC
Hi

LOT
Of course they were terrorists

SAHRAH
Did anyone die?

LOT
They're thugs and political opportunists / and they are about as holy as a
    pack of jackals

EDITH
There are many factions, you can't lump them all together
Besides, we have family in the / insurgency, your own *son-in-law*

SAHRAH
Give it up, Mom, you're not going to win this one

EDITH
They are fighting for our freedom and for, for / our political autonomy;
    they are not—

LOT
Just see how much freedom you'll have if they win

EDITH
a pack of jackals, I mean our own doctor is fighting for them, for heaven's sake

LOT
Oh well then they *must* be righteous warriors

SAHRAH
Mom, just—

A baby starts crying. SAHRAH *exits to tend to it.*

LOT
You can be sure this is just the thunder before the storm

EDITH
Everyone's nerves were rattled but the afternoon wore on
more or less like a regular Sunday
Lot was glued to the television of course
waiting for any mention of the car bomb
I had no stomach for the gruesome details
I made a nice lunch for everyone
The babies were messy tyrants as usual
Splatting sauce and juice absolutely everywhere
And then . . . I was outside taking the laundry down off the line
when I heard voices in the living room
One of the babies was crying
I walked in with the laundry basket and . . .

Lights up on DEREK *and* CHRIS *in full American military fatigues.*
CHRIS's *leg is severely injured.*

LOT
Two angels have come to pay us a visit
God bless you both; you are angels sent from God
Bringing order to this chaos
Risking your lives

EDITH
I noticed the "angels" hadn't thought to take off their muddy boots before
    walking into my house
And then I noticed one of them was injured

LOT
One of them is injured

EDITH
Yeah, I can see that

LOT
I think from the car bomb

EDITH
Don't they have some kind of field hospital?

LOT
A what?

EDITH
Or a helicopter to pick them up?

LOT
Well I don't know, obviously not if they're asking us for help

EDITH
The angels were trying to explain what happened
But they didn't speak our language
so it was very hard to understand what exactly they needed
Which, frankly, irritated me
I mean here you are in my country
The least you could do if you're killing my neighbours is learn our language

LOT
(to CHRIS) Here, just sit down and we'll see what / we can do—

EDITH
Ah ah ah ah, not on the pullout bed!

LOT
Edith—

EDITH
He's covered in blood!
Put him on the kitchen chair

> *LOT sits CHRIS down on a kitchen chair.*

LOT
Get a knife

EDITH
I don't feel comfortable with this

LOT
Edith—

EDITH
I don't want these men in my house
I don't feel comfortable

LOT
He's injured, for Christ's sake
he might die if we don't help him

EDITH
I'm not touching them

LOT
Sahrah!

> *Lights up on SAHRAH.*

We need your help with this
Grab a knife so we can cut away his pant leg

> *SAHRAH fetches and returns with a knife. LOT makes to take it from her, but she holds onto it.*

SAHRAH
I can do it myself

> *SAHRAH cuts away the bloody pant leg.*

DEREK
(as if to a child) Do you have any gauze?

SAHRAH
What?

> *DEREK mimes wrapping gauze around his leg.*

LOT
Something to cover his wound—

SAHRAH

Yes, obviously that is the next logical step
Does he think I'm an idiot?

SAHRAH fetches a bottle of alcohol and a few old dishcloths.

She rolls up one of the dishcloths and hands it to DEREK, who doesn't know what to do with it. SAHRAH mimes putting it in her mouth, as a gag.

DEREK

(smiling) Nah that's okay, he doesn't need it

SAHRAH pours a healthy dose of alcohol onto one of the cloths and administers it to CHRIS's leg.

CHRIS screams and writhes in agony. DEREK places the rolled-up cloth in CHRIS's mouth for him to chomp down on. SAHRAH then rips the remaining cloth into strips and wraps the strips around the wound. As SAHRAH wraps the wound, EDITH speaks.

EDITH

This was quite a usual scene: three men standing back
watching Sahrah do something more effectively than they could
She came out of the womb saying, "I can do it myself"
When the nurse went to cut her umbilical cord, Sahrah reached for the scissors
and said, "Thanks, but I can take care of this"
When I pushed her on the swings she would cry and scream
She wanted to pump her own legs
She wanted to swing herself thank you very much
When she was three I tried to tie her shoelaces
and she said, "I know five ways to tie shoes, Mom"
I was astounded . . . I only knew one

SAHRAH finishes up the wrapping.

SAHRAH
Now what?

LOT
You must be hungry

SAHRAH
Dad

    LOT mimes eating.

LOT
Food?
Do you want to eat?

EDITH
I could've punched him in the nose
(to LOT) I'm not making them dinner

CHRIS
If you had some coffee that would be fucking amazing

    CHRIS mimes drinking a coffee. SAHRAH pours him a glass of the liquor
    and hands it to him.

Thanks

DEREK
How are you doing?

CHRIS
I feel like shit

EDITH
I want them to go

DEREK
The wife's a bit of a ball-breaker, huh?

LOT
Let him rest for a moment

DEREK
The husband's / chill though

EDITH
The world is full of places to rest!
My kitchen is not the only one

CHRIS
Yeah, I like him

LOT
Dinner would be the hospitable thing to do

DEREK
Did you check out the daughter's ass?

EDITH
You mean for me to do

CHRIS
Brah, my fucking leg was gushing blood
No, I didn't check out her ass

DEREK
Grade A sirloin

> LOT *mimes eating once more.*

LOT
You want to eat?

SAHRAH
Dad

DEREK
That would be awesome
(nodding) Yes, thank you

EDITH
(to LOT) I could wring your neck, you know that?

CHRIS
My leg is on fire

DEREK
They'll get you fixed up

EDITH
I don't even think we have enough food

SAHRAH
They look like they eat a lot

CHRIS
I think I'll probably end up losing it

DEREK
Nah, I've seen / worse

CHRIS
Yeah, but we'll probably be stranded out here for five or six fucking hours

DEREK
No

CHRIS
Damn straight—

A jolt of pain.

—AH *fuck*

    DEREK indicates to CHRIS and the pullout couch.

DEREK
Can my friend lie down?
Is it okay if he—

LOT
Yes yes—

EDITH
Not on the—

    *DEREK lays CHRIS down on the pullout couch. EDITH closes her eyes in
exasperation.*

LOT
Do we have an extra pillow?

EDITH
No, we don't

DEREK
You good?

CHRIS
Yeah

DEREK
She's pissed, eh?
The wife

CHRIS
Fuck her

SAHRAH
(to LOT) So what was all this about no male visitors?
And the neighbours?
How many do you think saw you taking them in?

CHRIS
(referring to SAHRAH) Goddamn

DEREK
You see what I'm saying?

CHRIS
I'd like to get into that

DEREK
I'd like to see you try, gimpy

> CHRIS *chuckels.*

CHRIS
Fuck off

EDITH
Did these two idiots think that a mother
doesn't know when a man is leering at her daughter?
No matter the language
a mother always knows when you are leering at her daughter
If I didn't leave right then I was going to cut their balls off
I put on my shawl and headed for the door

LOT
Where are you going?

EDITH
We're out of salt

LOT
Salt?

EDITH
It's a cooking ingredient

LOT
But the market's closed

EDITH
I know
I shop there every day

Lights fade on the others.

By this point I just wanted the day to be over
I felt exhausted
I just didn't have the energy that I used to
Especially not for unexpected visits
Plus I struggle a bit from anxiety
Disturbances from my routine can really set me off
I get that from my mother's side
Lot is completely insensitive to it of course
I wish you could have seen him when he was a young man
He could be quite thoughtful in his way

I knocked on my neighbour Nasra's door
Nasra and I were in the same book club, but I didn't like her very much
She was just a bit mean-spirited, you know?
Always found the negative in everything
Those kinds of people can just wear you down
At any rate, she came to the door and I asked her for a cup of salt
She could see that I was worn out and she asked what was wrong

and so I told her about our guests and the car bomb and the injury and . . .
And you know I probably ended up saying more than I needed to
but by that point I was tired and irritable and just needed someone to vent to
And to her credit she was very understanding
and gave me a nice full cup of salt

And as I walked back across the street
I passed another neighbour, on his way home
and I also happened to mention our visitors
and he was quite shocked by the whole scenario
and sympathized with my irritation completely, and, in fact
appeared very upset that they were in our village at all
I mean, a lot of people had very strong feelings about what was going on
Which I didn't blame them for in the least

> *Lights fade back up on the others.* ISAAC *is helping* SAHRAH *prepare dinner.*

When I walked back into the house
the three of them were blathering to each other

LOT
What's your name?

DEREK
What?

> LOT *points to himself.*

LOT
Lot

CHRIS
Is that your name?

DEREK
Lot?

LOT
Lot, yes

CHRIS
Lot

DEREK
Derek

LOT
Derek?

DEREK
You got it

CHRIS
Chris

    LOT chuckles.

LOT
Okay

    DEREK chuckles in recognition of "okay."

DEREK
Okay

CHRIS
Yeah, brah, everything's gonna be okay

DEREK
Thanks for the help, Lot

CHRIS
Yeah, thanks a lot

The soldiers laugh. LOT *smiles but obviously does not understand.*

Man, they don't speak a word of fucking English, do they?

DEREK
How's that even possible?
I mean they got a TV and everything

EDITH
(to SAHRAH) I don't like how that one is looking at you

SAHRAH
He wishes

EDITH
Yeah well be careful
what angels want they take by force

SAHRAH
Momma

EDITH
You're too young to remember the first war

Lights fade on the others once more, leaving just EDITH *illuminated.*

With Isaac's help, Sahrah and I pulled a fast meal together
With Nanna and the babies there were nine of us crammed into the house
balancing plates and cups on our knees
no one really knowing what to say
just the sound of knives and forks and the television
One of the angels kept listening to his helmet
waiting for some kind of message from God

about when they were going to be picked up by their helicopter
or whatever was coming for them
when suddenly he stood up as if sensing something
and then—

   The sound of banging on a door.

This next part happened so fast I—
I was sitting farthest from the door, closest to the kitchen
and out the window I saw the heads of eight or nine men
banging on the door and shouting something
I couldn't make it out because the babies were screaming
and as Sahrah jumped up she knocked my arm and my plate went flying

   EDITH *laughs.*

all over Nanna, I shouldn't laugh
And I had a drink of some kind, anyway that was kicked over
And when I looked up Lot was at the door
trying to calm the crowd saying, "I have a daughter, she has babies, please"
and I just remember hands—this wall of hands
and he's pulled into the crowd like this—by the front of his shirt
And one of the angels is holding his gun—this huge black gun
which I had had my eyes on all night like
I had the feeling that gun was staring into my soul all night
and then the gun opened its mouth

   She opens her mouth wide.

and screamed
into my ceiling, bullets through the plate I'm holding
it shatters in my hand, my hands are bleeding
a glass explodes on the ground, Nanna on the ground
slumped forward at this point, bleeding slumped
slumped on the ground by the glass I'm, I'm in the dark
I'm in the dark on the ground at the back of the house hiding

my face down, in the ground hiding, hands bleeding, shaking, the baby screaming
I reach in the dark and my hand touches a hand and it squeezes back   Isaac?
Yes
It's Isaac's hand
I'm on the floor with Isaac
Sahrah?

A faint light appears on SAHRAH.

SAHRAH
Nanna's dead

EDITH
Are you / okay?

SAHRAH
Nanna's dead

EDITH
I know, sweetie, where's your father?

SAHRAH
I don't know

EDITH
Is he—?

SAHRAH
Down the street

EDITH
Down / the—?

SAHRAH
In the street

EDITH
I try to stand up, but I can't I can't bend my leg
there's a shard of glass in my knee, right at the bend
right in the socket, and I pull it out
And then, okay, then I can stand
I walk into the kitchen and I look out the window
and I can see the crowd—it's bigger than I thought
and there's an old blue pick-up truck
with five or six men riding in the back
and they're pulling something, behind the truck
pulling something through the street
away from me and then turning at the end of the street
then pulling it back towards the house
towards me, and I can see it's one of the soldiers
and his leg is gone—in fact his face too
his face is gone, it's been erased
and I can't tell if he's alive, but I hope not
for his sake, and oh I should say he's naked
no clothes—everything—stripped off, bare
to the muscle in parts as they drag him
bare right down to the bone eventually
though I don't watch that long

They burned their flag too
I never understood that
Where did they get the flag?
I hated them, but not like that

Of course they filmed it and put it online
After the window—I can't remember
The smell of gas and smoke . . .

Lot came back
His nose was broken

Lights up faintly on LOT, *bleeding profusely from his nose.*

SAHRAH tends to him—she wipes away the blood and then hands him a cloth to hold over his nose. She pours him a shot of alcohol and he knocks it back.

LOT
Jackals

EDITH
And then he saw his mother on the ground
He knelt beside her
and, for the first time in his life
he wept

    Beat.

Sahrah picked up a broom
out of the broken glass
and swept

LOT
Stop—just—

SAHRAH
Don't talk to / me

LOT
Do you feel no sadness for / your grandmother?

SAHRAH
Of course I feel sadness

LOT
You have a funny way of showing it

SAHRAH
Who is going to clean this house?
God?
Is God going to clean this house?
Lord knows you won't

> *LOT stands up to confront her and SAHRAH begins beating him with her fists.*

Stupid stupid stupid / stupid stupid stupid stupid . . .

EDITH
(overtop) Stop it STOP IT, both of you!

> *SAHRAH breaks down sobbing.*

> *LOT sits down.*

> *The sound of a baby crying.*

> *SAHRAH exits—her light goes out.*

> *A long moment passes between husband and wife.*

And then, the young angel returned

> *Lights up on DEREK. There is a massive, bloody gash across his face. He is filthy.*

His gun was gone
Where could his gun have gone?
And his helmet too
He looked at Lot and then looked at me
back down at Lot and then back up at me
And then he walked right up to me
and stared into my eyes

like his gun had looked at me
but this time with his real eyes
his real eyes were like two little gems
He was trembling
He was a boy
My God, this was not an angel, this was a boy

DEREK
It's very important you listen carefully to what / I'm about to say, alright?

EDITH
I can't understand what you're saying

DEREK
There are going to be drone strikes hitting your village, alright?
Very soon
They are going after targets all around / your home
After what happened they're going to rain down like God's wrath
You understand what I'm saying?

EDITH
I'm sorry—I-I can't understand

DEREK
You have to take your family and you have to go—

    DEREK points off into the distance repeatedly.

You have to *go*
Do you understand?
You have to *go*

EDITH
Go?

DEREK
Yes
Yes you have to go *now*
and don't look back

    Lights out on DEREK.

EDITH
What do you think he said?

LOT
I think he wants us to leave

EDITH
Our house?

LOT
The village I think

EDITH
And go where?

LOT
I don't know

EDITH
Tonight?

LOT
We have to bury Nanna

EDITH
Yes

LOT
I should—call relatives

EDITH
Yes of course

LOT
The proper arrangements should be made

> *LOT turns to leave.*

> *A moment.*

> *LOT reconsiders.*

I think he means for us to get out / right now

EDITH
I think we need to go now

LOT
Sahrah!

EDITH
Where's Isaac?

> *Lights up on SAHRAH.*

SAHRAH
Are they back?

EDITH
We have go

SAHRAH
Where?

EDITH
Isaac!

LOT
Into the desert

Lights up on ISAAC.

EDITH
They're going to strike

SAHRAH
How do / you know?

LOT
Let's go / let's go let's go

ISAAC
Where are we going?

EDITH
We'll figure / out, just hurry

SAHRAH
How do you know there'll be / strikes?

EDITH
Because he told / us

ISAAC
What should we bring?

LOT
There's no time—

SAHRAH
How long are we / going to be?

LOT
—-just leave everything, we gotta *go*!

SAHRAH
Alright just calm the fuck down Dad I need to put on my sandals

EDITH
She was holding her first-born and she passed her to me
She asked Isaac to grab her second
And he asked where she was

SAHRAH
You had her

ISAAC
Me?

SAHRAH
You were holding her when the shooting started

ISAAC
No I wasn't

SAHRAH
I saw her in your / hands

ISAAC
That was my sweater

SAHRAH
I thought *you had her*

ISAAC
I'm sorry

SAHRAH
Where's my baby?

> *During EDITH's monologue a light remains on SAHRAH. They fade on all of the others.*

EDITH
She started tearing through the house
screaming for her baby
I held her first-born in my arms
but the second one—we couldn't hear where she was
Where's my baby? Where's my baby?!
Sahrah was—

> *EDITH struggles to keep composure.*

Of course Sahrah was not screaming "where's my baby?"
She was calling her baby by her name
She was of course calling her beautiful child by her beautiful—

> *EDITH breaks down.*

But for the purposes of this . . . recounting
I will call her "baby" because . . . I cannot
say her name, I cannot say . . .

> *She shakes her head.*

My daughter was calling for her daughter
my granddaughter
she was calling for my granddaughter by her name but she was not there
She was not there
I don't know
She was gone

> *EDITH falters.*

The sound . . .
To hear your own daughter . . .
To hear your child . . .
The sound she made . . .
This wail inside, *deep* inside her
like her soul was tearing her—
I could hear her tearing apart
Quite literally I heard it happen
I said, "Sahrah, we have to go"
She said no
She said . . .

EDITH sobs.

I will not leave my baby
I have to find my baby
I said, "Sahrah, we have to go, there's no time"
Lot and Isaac were up the street shouting
and Sahrah . . . she kept—no no no no
I will not leave my baby I will not leave her
I will not leave her
I will not leave her
Under the couch
Under the bed
The backyard
Cupboards
I will not leave her
Under the couch again
Sahrah throwing couch cushions
emptying the closet, the cabinets
dishes on the floor
That is how I left her
A storm inside the house
I said, "I love you"
I said I love you
. . . and I closed the door

The light slowly fades on SAHRAH.

And then I ran, her first-born in my arms
I ran past Nasra's house
past the houses of my neighbours
and my neighbours' neighbours
I ran through the market all boarded up for the night
I tried to shout: *(whispers)* run!
But my heart was broken
I couldn't make a sound
As I ran through the streets I thought:
"I certainly didn't think Sunday would turn out like this"

I saw Lot and Isaac up ahead
nearing the edge of town
I ran hard and closed the gap
until my knee—I felt it catch
the fleck of glass still lodged there
and I buckled; I tumbled face down into the ground
fell hard, chipped a tooth, and the baby, she hit the ground hard too
I looked up and saw Isaac running back
I saw Isaac running back, sweet Isaac
He came back for me and the baby, I said, "Take her, take the baby"
and he did and he helped me to my feet, but I was limping now
I apologized to him that this had been such a chaotic visit
Next time we'll go to the water park, I said

He pulled me along for a while until I said *go*
just go and they ran off and I kept going
first at a jog and then pushing through the pain
I broke back into a run and suddenly I felt white—
I felt whiteness, white light from behind me
like sunrise or a photograph and then the blast
the crack of thunder and the earth shook and
knocked me to my knees but I staggered up
as the flames licked the night and then more white light

more thunder and the sulphurous smell
of God's wrath raining down from the sky
sucking the air with it, sucking it from my lungs
darkness from the heavens
and scorching gravel and dead birds
And still I ran on, the heat at my back
and in the distance, silhouetted against the desert
a boy carrying my granddaughter
and beyond them, my husband, carried by his fear

The night was purple and it was the colour of her face
the moment she came out of me, the umbilical cord around her neck
the midwife said she would not see morning
They said she was dead, but I said no
I will not leave her
I held her in my arms all night and prayed to God
to breathe life into her lungs
I said I love you and kissed her soft head
softer than the skin of an eyelid
And as morning came they tried to take you away from me again
but I said no—
I will not leave you
I placed the tip of my finger
into your whole hand
I placed . . . just . . . the tippiest tip of my finger into your hand
And I felt it slowly close
I felt your hand slowly close around my fingertip
And then you opened your eyes
You opened your eyes and you looked into mine

And then . . . I stopped running
The darkness ahead of me and the fire behind me
I stopped running because I had to know if you were behind me
I had to know if you had made it out
Because what was I running towards if you hadn't?

So yes, I stopped
And yes, I looked back
I looked back to see if you had made it out
I looked back to see your face

For the first time in the entire play EDITH *moves: she looks back.*

Blackout.

End of play.

ACKNOWLEDGEMENTS

My sincerest thanks to everyone at Canadian Stage who first gave life to these plays. To Matthew Jocelyn, Sherrie Johnson, and Birgit Schreyer Duarte for first believing in them. To my two brave directors, Matjash Mrozewski and Estelle Shook. To our fearless and peerless cast: Salvatore Antonio, Nicola Correia-Damude, Christopher Morris, Alon Nashman, Valerie Buhagiar, and Stephen Jackman-Torkoff. And to our incredible production team: James Lavoie, Steve Lucas, Samuel Sholdice, Cameron Davis, Simon Fon, Michael Sinclair, Andrea Baggs, Bryan Steele, Vanessa Janiszewski, Peter Velocci, Melanie Hall, and Ming Wong. Further thanks to Colin Rivers, Michael Levine and the Brian Linehan Charitable Foundation, the Canada Council for the Arts, the Ontario Arts Council, and the Toronto Arts Council.

Plays seldom get such a beautiful *renaissance* than the one offered to *Botticelli in the Fire* by Woolly Mammoth Theatre. It would never have happened without the vision and trust of Howard Shalwitz, Kirsten Bowen, and Leora Morris. Nor without my comrade-in-arms, Marti Lyons, and our exquisite cast: Jon Hudson Odom, Alyssa Wilmoth-Keegan, Cody Nickell, Earl T. Kim, Craig Wallace, Dawn Ursula, and James Crichton. I am also indebted to our superb production team: Misha Kachman, Ivania Stack, Colin K. Bills, Christian Frederickson, Kirsten Bowen, Robb Hunter, Lorraine Ressegger-Slone, Rachael Danielle Albert, Robyn Rikoon, Leigh Robinette, Jennifer Sheetz, Joel Garcia, Charlotte Cugnini, and Jenn Harris.

I cannot speak highly enough of the entire team at Playwrights Canada Press. To Annie Gibson and Blake Sproule in particular: thank you again for making a beautiful book with me. Your hard work enriches our theatrical ecology immensely.

I am indebted to Wisława Szymborska, whose poem "Lot's Wife" inspired several lines in Edith's monologue in *Sunday in Sodom*.

I offer my immeasurable gratitude to my family, my friends, and my love, James.

Finally, I want to pay homage to the queers who have fought the good fight, and the hard fight, throughout history. And to those who will continue to shine the light in the dark days to come.

Jordan Tannahill is a playwright, author, and filmmaker. Jordan's plays have been translated into multiple languages and honoured with various prizes, including the Governor General's Literary Award for Drama, the John Hirsch Prize, and multiple Dora Mavor Moore Awards. In the last year, Jordan's play *Late Company* transferred to London's West End; his virtual-reality piece *Draw Me Close* premiered at the Venice Biennale; his debut novel *Liminal* was published by House of Anansi; he premiered his play *Declarations* at Canadian Stage; and he collaborated with Akram Khan on *Xenos*, currently touring internationally. Visit www.jordantannahill.com.

First edition: September 2018. Second printing: February 2019.
Printed and bound in Canada by Imprimerie Gauvin, Gatineau.

Jacket design by James March
Jacket art, a detail of *The Birth of Venus*, by Sandro Botticelli
Author photo © Alejandro Santiago

PLAYWRIGHTS
CANADA PRESS
202-269 Richmond St. W.
Toronto, ON
M5V 1X1

416.703.0013
info@playwrightscanada.com
www.playwrightscanada.com
@playcanpress